Cambridge Elements

Elements in Forensic Linguistics
edited by
Tim Grant
Aston University
Tammy Gales
Hofstra University

DOXXING DISCOURSE

Carmen Lee
The Chinese University of Hong Kong

Shaftesbury Road, Cambridge CB2 8EA, United Kingdom

One Liberty Plaza, 20th Floor, New York, NY 10006, USA

477 Williamstown Road, Port Melbourne, VIC 3207, Australia

314–321, 3rd Floor, Plot 3, Splendor Forum, Jasola District Centre,
New Delhi – 110025, India

Cambridge University Press is part of Cambridge University Press & Assessment,
a department of the University of Cambridge.

We share the University's mission to contribute to society through the pursuit of
education, learning and research at the highest international levels of excellence.

www.cambridge.org
Information on this title: www.cambridge.org/9781009518727
DOI: 10.1017/9781009518734

© Carmen Lee 2026

This publication is in copyright. Subject to statutory exception and to the provisions
of relevant collective licensing agreements, no reproduction of any part may take
place without the written permission of Cambridge University Press & Assessment.

When citing this work, please include a reference to the DOI 10.1017/9781009518734

First published 2026

A catalogue record for this publication is available from the British Library

ISBN 978-1-009-51872-7 Hardback
ISBN 978-1-009-51876-5 Paperback
ISSN 2634-7334 (online)
ISSN 2634-7326 (print)

Cambridge University Press & Assessment has no responsibility for the persistence
or accuracy of URLs for external or third-party internet websites referred to in this
publication and does not guarantee that any content on such websites is, or will remain,
accurate or appropriate.

For EU product safety concerns, contact us at Calle de José Abascal, 56, 1°, 28003
Madrid, Spain, or email eugpsr@cambridge.org

Doxxing Discourse

Elements in Forensic Linguistics

DOI: 10.1017/9781009518734
First published online: February 2026

Carmen Lee
The Chinese University of Hong Kong
Author for correspondence: Carmen Lee, carmenlee@cuhk.edu.hk

Abstract: Doxxing is the deliberate, unauthorized disclosure of personal information, often with malicious intent. Notably, it became a key method of public shaming and vigilantism during the 2019–2020 Hong Kong protests. This Element understands and examines doxxing as a discursive practice. Using critical discourse analysis (CDA), it analyzes online forum discussions, survey and interview data from Hong Kong university students. Findings are examined alongside institutional legal texts to show how doxxing is discursively constructed, legitimized, and contested by different social actors. The case study identifies linguistic strategies such as metaphor, euphemism, and irony, along with legitimation discourses framing doxxing as social justice, deterrence, or moral self-defense. The Element also problematizes legal ambiguities and ethical tensions surrounding doxxing practices. By foregrounding the interplay between grassroots and legal discourses, it contributes to forensic linguistics scholarship on digital harm, power, and morality in contemporary mediated environments.

Keywords: doxxing, critical discourse analysis, (de-)legitimation, digital vigilantism, morality

© Carmen Lee 2026

ISBNs: 9781009518727 (HB), 9781009518765 (PB), 9781009518734 (OC)
ISSNs: 2634-7334 (online), 2634-7326 (print)

Contents

	Series Preface	1
1	What Is Doxxing?	1
2	Researching Doxxing as a Discursive Action	7
3	Language and Discourse Strategies of Doxxing Discussions Online	18
4	Attitudes and Perceptions Toward Doxxing	34
5	The Doxxing Law: Institutional Representations and Public Interpretations	45
6	Conclusions and Implications	58
	Appendix	67
	References	72

Doxxing Discourse 1

Series Preface

The Elements in Forensic Linguistics series from Cambridge University Press publishes across five main topic areas (1) investigative and forensic text analysis; (2) the study of spoken linguistic practices in legal contexts; (3) the linguistic analysis of written legal texts; (4) Interdisciplinary research in related fields; (5) Historical development and reflection often through explorations of the origins, development and scope of the field in various countries and regions. *Doxxing Discourse* by Carmen Lee provides a sociolegal and ethical study of the practice of 'doxxing', of openly documenting or revealing a hidden identity, in the context of the Hong Kong extradition protest movements 2019–2020. In this context, Lee argues that doxxing becomes conceptualised as an attempt at public shaming individuals from the policing and security forces.

Taking a critical discourse studies approach this Element examines doxxing, as a discursive action and through a variety of standpoint examines the construction of the doxxing by those who are engaging in the activity, as well as by the media and official and legal standpoints. As doxxing of police and security officers became criminalised in the Hong Kong context this Element sets out how the act of doxxing was the legitimated and justified by those engaging in the activity. This clash between the legal constructions and the protester constructions provides a picture of a fascinating struggle over the notion of public interest, and in turn a new ideological take on the debate between everyday and legal meanings.

This Element then takes the local context of the 2019–2020 Hong Kong protests and through this opens out debates that may become increasingly relevant as doxxing might become a tactic for consideration in other jurisdictions, where policing, legal and executive powers attract potential resistance and protest. It makes an exciting addition to the series.

Tim Grant
Series Editor

1 What Is Doxxing?

During the 2019–2020 anti-extradition bill protests in Hong Kong, the personal data of thousands of police officers were published on various social media and online forums. Protesters and bystanders have described these actions as seeking justice in response to police violence against protesters at the protest sites. Similar incidents of doxxing have unfolded across the globe in recent years. In China, a high-profile case in March 2025 involved the thirteen-year-old daughter of Baidu's vice president allegedly doxxing a pregnant woman during an online dispute about a K-pop star, resulting in the disclosure of her workplace details and incidents of online harassment targeting the woman's family.[1] Around the same time, the website Dogequest disclosed the personal information of Tesla owners and employees of the Department of Government Efficiency (DOGE) in protest against Elon Musk, which was followed by incidents of vandalism against Tesla properties.[2]

These are incidents of what is now known as *doxxing*, defined as the act of deliberately seeking and publishing someone's personal information without their consent, often with malicious intent, such as shaming or punishing targets for their alleged wrongdoings. The information disclosed can include doxxed targets' names, home and work addresses, phone numbers, financial records, and other sensitive data. The term "doxxing" (or "doxing") originates from "docs," short form for "documents." The phrase "dropping documents" or "dropping dox" was a form of revenge in 1990s hacker culture. It involved uncovering and exposing the identity of people who fostered anonymity (Douglas, 2016, p. 200). Today, one does not need to be a hacker to collect and expose others' personal data. With people massively sharing their own lives online, their personal information can be easily gathered and disclosed by others. Victims of doxxing can extend beyond the original targets to their families, friends, and related social networks.

Douglas (2016) classifies doxxing into three major categories: *deanonymizing* doxxing, the release of personal information to reveal the identity of a formerly anonymous individual; *targeting* doxxing, the disclosure of personal information that locates the target's physical location or contact details, which were previously private; and *delegitimizing* doxxing, revealing intimate personal information that damages the reputation of an individual. Building on Douglas' categorization, Anderson and Wood (2021) provide a finer-grained typology of doxxing based on motives and the types of loss and harm caused to victims. The seven mutually nonexclusive motivations are:

(i) *Extortion doxxing*: disclosing or threatening to disclose someone's personal information in order to gain financial or other benefits.
(ii) *Silencing doxxing*: doxxing to intimidate someone into withdrawing from an online forum or silencing them from participating in the discussion.
(iii) *Retribution doxxing*: a common type of doxxing motivated by a desire to punish someone for perceived wrongdoings. The four incidents described at the beginning of this Section are to different extents forms of retribution.

---

[1] www.thestandard.com.hk/market/article/71027/Red-faced-Baidu-VP-apologizes-over-daughters-doxxing-offenses.
[2] www.nbcnews.com/tech/internet/tesla-dogequest-website-owner-list-dox-site-link-rcna197112.

(iv) *Controlling doxxing*: this type of doxxing aims to manipulate targets' behavior. This is commonly used in the context of coercive control within intimate partner violence.
(v) *Reputation-building doxxing*: skillfully collecting and publishing personal data to gain acceptance within a group or subculture. For instance, a hacker might doxx a competitor to demonstrate their hacking skills to earn respect within the hacker community.
(vi) *Unintentional doxxing*: doxxing that occurs without malicious intent, often due to carelessness or lack of privacy awareness.
(vii) *Public interest doxxing*: doxxing driven by the belief that disclosing personally identifiable or sensitive information serves the public good. For example, publishing the identities of those involved in corruption to hold them accountable.

As can be seen, not all instances of doxxing are motivated by malice. Despite its potential to cause psychological or physical harm to victims, doxxing has been used as a tool for social justice and morality. In mainland China, the Human Flesh Search Engine (人肉搜尋), that is, netizens collectively gathering and publishing targets' personal information, has reportedly uncovered such illegal acts as corruption of government officials, resulting in doxxed targets being fired or arrested (Gao, 2016).

Defining doxxing is not a straightforward matter, especially when it comes to journalistic reporting of personal data in the interest of the public. In December 2022, Elon Musk accused a group of tech journalists of doxxing him by reporting on a Twitter account (@ElonJet) that tracked his private jet using publicly available data. As a result, Musk suspended the journalists' Twitter accounts. However, many argued that the journalists engaged in legitimate reporting and that Musk's banning of the journalists' accounts undermined freedom of expression (Mauran, 2022). This incident illustrates that on social media, the boundaries between doxxing and legitimate reporting become increasingly blurry, particularly when celebrities and public figures are involved.

1.1 Digital Vigilantism and Doxxing

Doxxing is closely linked to digital vigilantism, or digilantism, defined as "a process where citizens are collectively offended by other citizen activity, and coordinate retaliation on mobile devices and social platforms" (Trottier, 2017, p. 55). This "weaponised visibility" involves "naming and shaming" to expose, shame, and punish individuals, often resulting in enduring psychological and physical harm to targets. Those engaging in digilantism take justice into their own hands to address perceived wrongdoings.

The affordances of digital media – anonymity, global reach, and ease of sharing – have empowered ordinary web users to act as digilantes. Crucially, as society becomes increasingly mediatized and connected, one does not need to be a hacker to retrieve and share others' information publicly online. As soon as people post content to their social media profiles, whether it is intended to be shared privately or publicly, they are already exposing themselves to an unknown and unintended audience. For example, a "private" Facebook post intended for friends only can easily be reshared by a friend to an unexpected audience. This phenomenon is called the "context collapse" of social media, that is, the "collapse of infinite possible contexts" into one, with an "infinitely ambiguous audience" (Wesch, 2009, p. 23). The diminishing of contextual boundaries enables digilantes to weaponize everyday personal data. The widespread availability of personal data and the ease of sharing information have made doxxing a powerful tool for digilantes to achieve various purposes. In recent years, doxxing has become a common tactic for grassroots activism. For example, in the Hong Kong 2019–2020 protests, targets of political doxxing included politicians, activists, police officers, and journalists (Lee, 2020).

The impact of doxxing extends beyond privacy invasion to psychological distress, reputation damage, and even physical harm to the victims. Digital affordances, characterized by "spreadability" (ease of sharing and circulation), "searchability" (ability to search and find content), and "visibility" (ability to make content visible to specific audiences) (boyd, 2010, p. 43), make "forgetness" almost impossible, that is, the shared information remains accessible and visible indefinitely online (Garcés-Conejos Blitvich, 2022). The repeated resharing and persistent disclosure of personal information online can endanger victims and subject them to ongoing scrutiny.

1.2 Anti-Doxxing Laws

In response to the surge of doxxing cases in recent years, legal measures have been implemented in various countries and jurisdictions to regulate doxxing. While some jurisdictions rely on existing laws, others introduce new or amended legislation to prohibit doxxing offences.

In Australia, the Parliament passed the Privacy and Other Legislation Amendment Act 2024 under the Criminal Code Act 1995 to formally criminalize doxxing. This Act covers two new doxxing-related offences: one is for general doxxing, with a penalty of up to six years of imprisonment, and another is for doxxing based on protected characteristics such as race and religion, with a penalty of up to seven years in prison (Parliament of Australia, 2024).

The legal implications of doxxing in the United States are more complex and continue to be contested. Unlike some jurisdictions, there is currently no comprehensive federal anti-doxxing law, and the act of publishing someone's personal information is generally protected under the First Amendment. However, doxxing can lose constitutional protection when it constitutes "true threats" or involves "incitement to imminent lawless action" (Cremins, 2024). As of 2025, about twenty states have enacted specific anti-doxxing legislation with varying scope and definitions. However, there remain constitutional tensions as many state laws may conflict with First Amendment protections due to their broad scope. The US case demonstrates the typical and ongoing tension between protecting individuals' rights to privacy and preserving freedom of expression (for details, see Cremins, 2024).

In Hong Kong, the context of this study, an anti-doxxing law was introduced under the Personal Data (Privacy) Ordinance (PDPO) in response to the rise in doxxing cases during the 2019 protests. The law is enacted under a two-tier structure: (i) a summary offence for disclosing personal data without consent with intent to cause harm, liable to a fine of HK$100,000 and up to two years in prison (Section 64(3A)); and (ii) an indictable offence, whereby, in addition to what is stated in the first-tier offence, the disclosure causes harm. The offence is punishable by a maximum fine of HK$1,000,000 and up to five years of imprisonment (Section 64(3C)). The Privacy Commissioner for Personal Data (PCPD) has also been granted more power to investigate and prosecute doxxing offenders (PCPD, n.d.).

Many jurisdictions are yet to implement a specific anti-doxxing law. In some countries, existing laws have been updated to accommodate the changing landscape of technology that shapes online offences. The UK does not have any specific anti-doxxing law to date. Doxxing-related practices such as harassment and unauthorized personal data disclosure are prosecuted under existing laws, including the Protection from Harassment Act 1997, the Malicious Communications Act 1988, and the Data Protection Act 2018 (Crown Prosecution Service, 2024).

Even with these legal measures, applying the doxxing law in real cases remains a challenge. First, it is difficult to strike a balance between protecting individuals' privacy and people's right to free speech. In addition, the affordances of digital media, such as users communicating anonymously and sharing information across multiple platforms, have made it difficult to track down those truly responsible for malicious doxxing. A further complication involves the varying interpretations of legal terms like "intent" and "harm" between institutions and lay actors, sometimes even leading to redefinitions of doxxing that reframe and legitimize harmful actions, as will be demonstrated in Section 5.

1.3 Doxxing as a Social Practice: A Turn to Language and Discourse

The challenge in defining doxxing stems from its multifaceted nature, which is best understood through the lens of *social practice*. As Trottier (2017, p. 68) argues, doxxing as a tool of digilantism "should not be regarded as an aberration from other digital media practices, but instead located on a continuum of forms of user-led policing and citizenship." The leakage of Tesla employees' data by Dogequest described at the beginning of this Section exemplifies how data sharing is weaponized as a tool of protest and retribution under the name of public interest and social justice. In other words, doxxing is not an isolated phenomenon; rather, it is situated in a continuum of practices enacted and amplified by digital media affordances and digital cultural practices that encourage massive sharing and bottom-up policing.

A limited body of academic research has conceptualized and investigated doxxing as a behavioral, psychological, and ethical matter. Scholars from such disciplines as sociology, communication studies, law, psychology, and information science have examined the motives behind doxxing, the methods employed by doxxers, and the consequences and harm caused (Douglas, 2016; Trottier, 2017; Chen et al., 2019; Anderson & Wood, 2021; Cheung, 2021; Huey et al., 2025). Despite much of online doxxing being enacted through written comments or messages posted on digital platforms, little attention is paid to the role of language that shapes the phenomenon.

This Element is amongst the first to contribute a language and discourse perspective to the growing body of doxxing scholarship. It conceptualizes doxxing as a social practice primarily enacted, represented, and sustained through discourse (Lee, 2020). Drawing on insights from multiple analytical tools such as netnography, critical discourse analysis (CDA), and pragmatics, this Element aims to unpack the discursive construction of doxxing practices. It offers a comprehensive analysis of a range of discourse features surrounding doxxing. It also reveals how ordinary people and institutions construct, negotiate, and contest its meaning.

This Element is organized as follows: Section 2 outlines the theoretical underpinnings and methodological approaches for researching doxxing as language and discourse. Drawing on the case of doxxing in Hong Kong, Section 3 examines the linguistic and discourse strategies employed in doxxing-related online discussions. Sections 4 and 5 continue to explore attitudes and perceptions toward doxxing, as well as how it is interpreted by participants, based on survey and interview data. This Element also examines selected legal documents of doxxing to reveal the limitations of top-down legal and institutional discourses surrounding doxxing. Section 6 concludes the Element by reflecting on the theoretical, methodological, and policy implications of the study. By analyzing the discursive strategies and public perceptions of doxxing, the study seeks to offer insights into the intersection of language, power, and policy in digital landscapes.

2 Researching Doxxing as a Discursive Action

2.1 Doxxing Discourse: Insights from Critical Discourse Studies

Having established doxxing as a social practice in Section 1, the central argument of this section, and in this Element as a whole, is that doxxing should be understood as not just an online behavior, but also a *discursive action*. This is because doxxing and its related practices are primarily produced, circulated, and sustained through language and discourse. Michel Foucault's conceptualization of *discourse as a system of thought* that shapes social reality (Foucault, 1972) provides a framework for understanding doxxing as discourse. Foucault argues that discourse is not merely language, but it is also a system of power that produces and regulates knowledge, identities, and (un)acceptable behaviors. In view of this, doxxing can be understood as operating within such discursive systems, where the act of disclosing personal information becomes a "technology of power" (Foucault, 1971) to punish targets through public shaming, resistance, or silencing. For example, during the US Capitol riot in 2021, doxxing of rioters was used as a form of counter-discourse against far-right extremism, which was often framed through discourses of resistance. Foucault's conceptualization of power and discourse aligns with doxxing's dual role in both exposing those who participated in the riot and constructing collective identities (e.g., "defenders of democracy" vs. "threats to democracy") as the events unfolded.

The field of Critical Discourse Studies (CDS), or what is commonly referred to as Critical Discourse Analysis (CDA),[3] provides a suitable theoretical framework for examining doxxing because it views discourse as a social practice that both shapes and is shaped by the social actors, contexts, institutions, and social structures in which it occurs (Wodak, 2014, p. 303). CDS is also "problem oriented and interdisciplinary" in approach (Wodak &

---

[3] In this Element, CDS is an umbrella term for the broader interdisciplinary field of critical discourse research, encompassing theoretical frameworks and methodologies that critically examine discourse as a social practice embedded in power relations and ideologies. When the term "CDA" is used, it specifically refers to a methodological approach within CDS that provides tools and concepts for analyzing discourse data.

Meyer, 2009, p. 2), which makes it particularly relevant in understanding a complex social practice like doxxing. This Element understands discourses *of* and *about* doxxing through the lens of CDS, in that people's actions and attitudes toward doxxing and its related activities are shaped by the everyday discourse that we routinely encounter in online and offline communicative landscapes (Teo, 2000). As a method of analyzing language and discourse, CDA is a contextualized approach that examines how language is used to justify, legitimize, and normalize acts of publicly exposing personal information, thereby revealing the complex social dynamics that underpin the practice of doxxing.

Although to date there has been limited discourse analysis of doxxing (but see Lee, 2020), there is an established body of language-based research analyzing various linguistic dimensions of conflicts, aggression, and abusive behavior in digital media. For example, linguistic devices such as irony, metaphors, and nonstandard orthography are commonly employed in enacting flaming and hate speech online (Herring, 1999; Assimakopoulos et al., 2017). In addition to overtly aggressive linguistic markers such as profanity and racial slurs, scholars have also observed an emerging pattern of "covert hate speech," that is, utterances that do not carry explicitly offensive language while causing harm (Baider & Constantinou, 2020), such as dehumanizing metaphors like referring to refugees or immigrants as "mice" or "worms." At the macro-level of discourse practices, researchers adopt CDA to understand the strategic ways in which ideologies are represented through verbal aggression online. For example, a delegitimation strategy, such as rejecting the professionalism of certain social groups, is often employed to justify verbal abuse online (Kagan et al., 2019). Focusing on trolling, Hardaker (2013) identifies a range of covert discourse strategies, such as the strategy of "digress," that is, "straying away from the purpose of the discussion." These covert strategies may seem harmless on the surface, but can still cause emotional discomfort to targets and possibly lead to offline physical abuse.

A closely relevant body of work that informs this Element's focus on doxxing discourse is Garcés-Conejos Blitvich's (2021, 2022) extensive research on online public shaming (OPS). Through digital discourse analysis and netnographic approaches, Garcés-Conejos Blitvich (2022) discusses six cases of OPS in the United States involving the exposure of perceived racism against visible minorities, where doxxing is a key tactic. Informed by pragmatic theories of (im)politeness, Garcés-Conejos Blitvich argues that OPS reflects emotional and coercive impoliteness, where heightened emotions like anger and indignation are used to punish targets' perceived wrongdoings, which is racism in this case. The research reveals the important role of language for bottom-up social regulation and resistance. It also informs the understanding of the dynamics of doxxing for the research reported in this Element, which aims to examine the complex interplay between discourse, morality, and social justice in online environments.

In the context of digital media, CDA offers a toolkit for digital discourse researchers to scrutinize the complex power relationships among social actors in online public spaces. It also helps unpack the role of digital activism and counter-discourses online in shaping offline socio-political events. Notably, Social Media Critical Discourse Studies (SMCDS) is an emerging approach to discourse analysis that addresses the changing dynamics of discursive power in social media (Bouvier & Machin, 2020; KhosraviNik, 2023). SMCDS argues that social media has transformed the traditional power relationship between authors and readers, allowing for increased reader agency in engaging with and responding to political content through online commenting. SMCDS also examines how social media users actively consume and produce political discourse to influence public opinion and political discussions. This study also applies CDA to analyze online doxxing discourses, so as to uncover how netizens and bystanders use language to justify or normalize doxxing.

2.2 Intertextuality and Recontextualization

Doxxing is primarily constructed through *intertextuality*, as the act of publicly exposing an individual's personal information depends on doxxers' sourcing, organizing, disseminating, and resharing a range of texts from both online (e.g., targets' social media profiles) and offline (e.g., public records). Intertextuality, the ways in which texts echo, incorporate, and respond to previous texts and voices, is a core concept in CDS (Fairclough, 2003). The notion has been applied in a range of data types and contexts, including the discourse of online hate speech and racism, where speakers mobilize intertextual references to increase the authority of their own stance (Hodsdon-Champeon, 2010) or to perform what has been called "intertextual impoliteness" (Badarneh, 2020). Intertextuality also demonstrates the ways in which texts are inherently *historical*, in that a text always "responds to, reaccentuates, and reworks past texts" to "make history" (Fairclough, 1992, p. 270). The historicity and temporality of texts are particularly relevant to the current study of doxxing. To doxx someone is to create and recreate the target's personal history through the assemblage of prior discourses that may be publicly or privately available online or offline.

In digital media, intertextuality is amplified by social media affordances. Users become "intertextual operators" (Androutsopoulos, 2010) who effortlessly modify and appropriate texts across media platforms through copy-pasting, taking screenshots, forwarding, and resharing. Personal and other private information that was intended for private sharing on one platform can now be easily reappropriated and repurposed, reinforced by context collapse, as discussed in Section 1. This repurposing of texts is enabled by *recontextualization*, a process where social actions are represented and transformed by discourses in new contexts (van Leeuwen & Wodak, 1999; van Leeuwen, 2009). In digital media, recontextualization occurs when content is shared across platforms and adapted to fresh discursive settings (Androutsopoulos, 2014). Recontextualization plays a crucial role in digitally mediated socio-political protests, where semiotic resources are rapidly recontextualized and distributed across physical and online spaces (Khosravinik & Unger, 2016). In addition, social media's real name policy and users' limited privacy awareness further facilitate the unexpected circulation of personal data, contributing to the proliferation of doxxing (Wauters et al., 2014).

2.3 Discourse Strategies of Legitimation, Justification, and Argumentation

Another concept from CDS that informs the current study is *legitimation*. As previously noted, doxxing is a criminal offence in some regions, including Hong Kong, and may fall under data privacy laws elsewhere that do not have specific anti-doxxing legislation. Given this background, it is reasonable to expect that in online forums, those engaged in doxxing or doxxing-related practices, including active users and bystanders, may manipulate or strategically deploy their language to continue exposing others' personal information without appearing to engage in illegal activities. A CDA approach allows researchers to uncover covert discourse strategies that justify, legitimize, or even normalize the controversial, and at times legally ambiguous, behavior of doxxing.

Legitimation discourse, as defined by Reyes (2011, p. 782), refers to "the process by which speakers accredit or license a type of social behavior." Van Leeuwen (2007, p. 92) outlines four primary categories of legitimation discourse: authorization (reference to authority, figures, or tradition), moral evaluation (references to value systems), rationalization (references to goals and uses of institutionalized social action), and mythopoesis (narratives that reward legitimate actions). These categories were initially developed to understand top-down legitimation processes of institutional actions, based on the assumption that "[l]egitimation is always the legitimation of the practices of specific institutional orders," such as policy documents that justify compulsory education (Van Leeuwen, 2007, p. 92). However, legitimation strategies are equally applicable in grassroots contexts, where counter-discourses seek to resist or subvert mainstream institutional narratives (Feltwell et al., 2017).

Legitimation is closely tied to the discourse process of *justification*, which refers to the linguistic realization of "defensive reactions to implied or inferred accusations" (Wodak, 1990, p. 132). Both legitimation and justification rely on *argumentation strategies* that allow the speaker or writer to position themselves as unbiased actors, "free of prejudice or even as a victim" (Wodak, 1995, p. 8; see also Reyes, 2011). In CDA, argumentation involves providing reasons that serve to explain social actions in order to (de) legitimize them. Legitimation discourse is also goal-oriented. Reyes (2011) observes that one of the most common goals of legitimation is to seek approval or acceptance from others by presenting potentially controversial action as serving a wider group or community. This Element demonstrates how the legitimation of doxxing emerges as a meaningful strategy employed by both ordinary people and institutions.

Against this conceptual and theoretical backdrop, this Element examines the discursive nature of doxxing and its implications for forensic linguistics research. Using the 2019–2020 Hong Kong protests as a case study, the Element explores how doxxing practices are discursively represented and constructed in both online discussions and institutional documents. The overarching research questions guiding this inquiry are: *How do online participants, bystanders, and policymakers discursively construct, represent, and perceive doxxing? What are the implications of these discursive constructions for understanding and addressing doxxing?*

2.4 Context: The 2019–2020 Hong Kong Protests and Doxxing of Police Officers

In 2019–2020, shortly before the global spread of the COVID-19 pandemic, Hong Kong witnessed one of its largest socio-political movements in history. The anti-extradition law amendment bill protests (also known as the Anti-ELAB movement) were a year-long pro-democracy movement against the proposed amendment of an extradition bill that would allow transfer of fugitives to any jurisdiction that Hong Kong lacks a formal agreement with, including mainland China. This sparked widespread concerns over potential threats to Hong Kong's legal autonomy as a special administrative region of China. The movement is believed to be leaderless and self-organized mainly on digital communication via social media and mobile apps such as Telegram and traditional online forums like LIHKG (Lee, 2020).

Despite the formal withdrawal of the bill in October 2019, tensions between the protesters, the government, and the police continued to escalate. Riot police were criticized for using excessive force, such as tear gas and rubber bullets, to disperse the protesters.[4] The protesters urged the government to meet their five demands, which included establishing an independent commission of inquiry into police use of violence. Media reports also revealed certain police officers concealing their identification numbers and badges and covering up their faces while on duty on the protest sites.[5] When the police became unidentifiable, this lack of transparency made it challenging for protesters to file complaints against them.

As the tension between the activists and the police surged, numerous doxxing incidents emerged on online forums and social media, notably the Hong Kong-based forum LIHKG, where the personal information of numerous police officers and their families was exposed. As of the end of 2019, the Office of the Privacy Commissioner for Personal Data (PCPD) of Hong Kong received over 1,500 complaints that involved the doxxing of police officers and their families (PCPD, 2020). Information being disclosed includes their full names, phone numbers, home addresses, spouses' and children's names, and schools attended, and so on, which was published along with pictures of the targets extracted from their personal social media profiles (Forsyth, 2020). What followed was a series of public shaming and harassment of these officers and their families online and offline (SCMP, 2019). As a result, the High Court granted an interim injunction order to ban all unauthorized publishing or disclosure of the personal data of police officers and their families. For a while, a handful of doxxing-related posts were removed from LIHKG.

Doxxing in Hong Kong predates the rise of social media. However, it became more widespread during the 2019 protests. As a result, Hong Kong's legal framework surrounding doxxing has evolved significantly. Based on a preliminary review of 124 media reports on doxxing between 2015 and 2022, four key phases of doxxing in Hong Kong have been identified:

(i) *Early concerns (2015–2016)*: In 2015, the government called for restricting access to public registers to protect privacy. As the Legislative Council Election approached in 2016, there were increasing cases of doxxing identified. Hong Kong Privacy Commissioner Stephen Wong urged internet users to respect the privacy of individuals.

(ii) *Legal measures and academic research (2017–2018)*: In November 2017, a financial consultant was charged with using others' personal data in direct marketing without consent. Personal data obtained from public domains

---

[4] Amnesty International (2019).
[5] www.nytimes.com/2019/07/26/technology/hong-kong-protests-facial-recognition-surveillance.html.

were also protected under the Personal Data (Privacy) Ordinance (PDPO). Academics also called for legal responses against cyberbullying. For example, Chen et al. (2018) noted that 30 percent of secondary school students had experienced doxxing.

(iii) *Protests (2019–2020)*: During the protests, several arrests were made for disclosing personal data of police officers and their family members. Notably, a thirty-two-year-old man was arrested for exposing the data of over 2,300 police officers on the Telegram channel "DadFindBoy" (Maragkou, 2019). In October 2019, an interim injunction was granted to ban doxxing against police officers and their families.

(iv) *Criminalization (2021 to date)*: The Personal Data (Privacy) (Amendment) Ordinance 2021 was passed on October 8, 2021, to criminalize doxxing. The first arrest under this law was made in December 2021 in which a thirty-one-year-old man was accused of posting the personal details of the victim with whom he had monetary feud.

2.5 Data Collection and Analysis

The data and analysis discussed in this Element are based on a research project funded by the Hong Kong government's Public Policy Research Funding Scheme (PPR project code: 2021.A4.075.21A). The original study examines how doxxing is defined, perceived, and justified online and among young people in Hong Kong, comparing these perspectives with legal and government definitions to inform education policy development that enhances critical awareness of doxxing. The research design for this study adopts a discourse-centred online ethnographic (DCOE) approach (Androutsopoulos, 2008), combining systematic observation of online discursive practices and insider perspectives from interviews with internet users. The study adopts a multi-staged design with four main phases of research activities:

PHASE 1: Contextualizing and Revealing Discourses of and about Doxxing

Prior to data collection, an extensive and up-to-date review of 124 media reports from various local newspapers in Hong Kong to understand how doxxing in the city evolved in recent years. With the introduction of the doxxing law in October 2021, reviewing news reports allowed the research team to gather timely and the most relevant empirical evidence of known doxxing cases in Hong Kong.

Following this preliminary review, a corpus of authentic online interactions was compiled from LIHKG (連登), a popular Hong Kong-based forum, known for its involvement in high-profile cases of cyberbullying and doxxing (SCMP, 2019). The primary language of data on LIHKG is Cantonese, a variety of Chinese spoken by over 90 percent of Hong Kong citizens. The forum is predominantly used by Hong Kongers and is often referred to as the Hong Kong version of Reddit or 4Chan (Wong, 2024). A keyword search for "起底" (doxxing) was conducted via the LIHKG search engine to identify relevant threads. The selection and review of threads focused on content that involved exposing personal data, categorized according to types of doxxing outlined by Douglas (2016) and Anderson & Wood (2021) – deanonymizing, targeting, delegitimizing, extortion, silencing, retribution, controlling, reputation-building, unintentional doxxing, and doxxing in the public interest.

The corpus consisted of forty-three threads and 28,943 comments. Two types of posts were collected:

- Name-and-shame incidents: These involve the disclosure of an individual's personal information for "naming and shaming."
- Reactive posts and comments to doxxing-related news: These posts and comments reflect users' attitudes and perceptions, providing insights into how doxxing is discussed and justified online.

These forum posts and comments illustrate how doxxing is discursively represented in their authentic context of communication. CDA is employed to unpack the implicit argumentation strategies that legitimize and justify doxxing. Analyzing the linguistic and discursive realizations of these posts reveals how doxxing is framed and how such discursive framing may be manipulated to legitimize doxxing in a covert manner. The aim of this qualitative discourse analysis is not to provide an exhaustive analysis of doxxing-related discourse or a single definition of doxxing. Instead, it seeks to offer a situated understanding of doxxing and reveal its fluidity and complexity. Given that the meaning of doxxing varies among users on LIHKG (Lee, 2020), the analysis focuses on how doxxing is (re)defined and justified by different social actors.

PHASE 2: Attitudes and Perceptions: Surveying and Interviewing University Students

Having obtained an informed and up-to-date understanding of the discursive nature of doxxing in Phase 1, Phase 2 of the study aimed to gather data on young people's attitudes and perceptions of doxxing. Undergraduate students from Hong Kong universities were chosen as participants for two reasons: (i) the limited research of doxxing in Hong Kong focuses primarily on teenagers (e.g., Chen et al., 2019); and (ii) university students were active participants in local online forums where doxxing incidents are evident (SCMP, 2019). Although these students may not have been directly involved in doxxing, it was reasonable to assume that they were aware of doxxing-related discussions before and after the social unrest.

An online questionnaire was administered to undergraduate students from different universities in Hong Kong to provide a snapshot of trends in their attitudes and perceptions. Our target respondents were all residents in Hong Kong, aged between 18 and 22. Members of this age group were chosen as they were the most active internet users (99.8 percent of penetration) according to HKSAR statistics in 2019. Although other age groups are equally vulnerable to doxxing, research has shown that young people are more likely to respond negatively to cyberbullying, such as self-harm and attempted suicide (John et al., 2018).

The questionnaire consisted of fifteen questions and took approximately 15–20 minutes to complete. It was hosted on the free survey service Qualtrics and distributed via university mass email services, personal contacts, and virtual class visits. By the end of March 2022, 500 respondents had completed the questionnaire.

The key set of questions takes reference from Assimakopoulos et al.'s (2017) questionnaire on perceptions of hate speech, which consists of the following parts:

(i) Likert scale ratings of selected definitions and statements about doxxing, so as to elicit respondents' perceptions of the issue;
(ii) Likert scale ratings of acceptability of authentic examples of doxxing discourse identified on LIHKG collected in Phase 1 of the study;
(iii) Multiple choice questions on respondents' overall experience with doxxing (e.g., whether they have been victims or perpetrators, or both);
(iv) Participants' level of understanding of the newly introduced doxxing law at the time and their rating of the clarity of the language used in the law.

Combining questionnaire and interviews has proven effective in much cyberbullying research to "capture broader perspectives and to pursue issues of interest with more targeted and in-depth questions" (Assimakopoulos et al., 2017, p. 20). Following the online survey, thirteen participants were invited to focus-group interviews to discuss their understanding and experience of doxxing. These participants agreed to be interviewed as indicated in their survey responses and were selected based on their survey answers to reflect a broad range of doxxing experiences and attitudes, so as to ensure a comprehensive analysis. The interview protocol was developed based on the research aims and the survey responses, focusing on discussions of participants' definitions of doxxing and reasons for their ratings.

As the study was conducted during COVID-19, all the interviews were conducted on Zoom as face-to-face meetings were not possible. Each focus group discussion lasted between sixty and ninety minutes. This was an initial discussion of participants' general perceptions of doxxing in Hong Kong. Additionally, five semi-structured individual interviews were conducted to follow up on specific themes emerging from the focus groups as well as specific survey responses. Participants were requested to share their first-hand experience as victims or perpetrators of doxxing upon their consent. Each interview lasted around sixty minutes. The combination of both focus-group and individual interviews enhances data richness by contextualizing the phenomenon under research and revealing specific themes in richer detail (Lambert & Loiselle, 2008). All of the interviews were conducted in Cantonese and recorded on Zoom.

Ethics clearance from the Chinese University of Hong Kong and informed consent from all participants were obtained. Participant identities are fully anonymized using pseudonyms (e.g., Respondent A, B, etc.) in this Element to prevent re-identification and potential exposure, particularly given the sensitive socio-political nature of the research context. To mitigate potential risk, research data were stored securely with limited access to the core research team members only.

PHASE 3: Analyzing Institutional Discourses of Doxxing

The third phase of the study examined how doxxing is represented in legal documents and government discourse. The aim is to compare institutional definitions with the discourses constructed by netizens and university students in the first two phases of the study. This comparative analysis serves to identify potential mismatches between the interpretation of doxxing among young people and institutional definitions, with the hope of facilitating more accurate and effective policy-making. A total of seventy-seven documents related to key doxxing cases in Hong Kong were collected, including:

- Fifty-three documents from government and PCPD publications, such as press releases on the PCPD website, documents and guidelines published by the Cyber Security and Technology Crime Bureau (CSTCB) of the Hong Kong Police Force, and resources published on the Education Bureau (EDB) website;
- Twenty-four legal and policy documents, the revised PDPO on doxxing, reports, and publications by The Law Reform Commission of Hong Kong and the Legislative Council.

2.6 Data Processing and Coding

The study adopted an iterative research process, where the research activities were constantly refined as the project progressed. Multiple data sources were triangulated to understand a particular theme from multiple perspectives. The *online questionnaire* results were generated through descriptive statistics. The purpose of the questionnaire findings is (i) to gain general insights into the participants' experience, perceptions, and attitudes of doxxing; (ii) to identify suitable participants for Phase 2 of the study; and (iii) to complement and contextualize the results of the qualitative discourse analysis in subsequent phases of the study. All the LIHKG posts, interview transcripts, and policy documents were imported to the qualitative analysis software MAXQDA to create a database of analyzable texts. Recordings of the interviews were transcribed verbatim by a student assistant. Codes were developed inductively from the data.

Coding and analysis were performed in two stages: The first was a thematic analysis. Following van Dijk's (2009) semantic macro-analysis, the research team performed both open and axial coding to identify salient themes and subcategories in the data. The second stage of coding paid close attention to the linguistic and discursive strategies using CDA tools and concepts. This phase of coding identified argumentation strategies related to the dissemination, legitimation, and naturalization of doxxing. This was achieved through repeated close and critical readings of the linguistic and content choices made in the LIHKG data, the interviews, and policy documents. The CDA was primarily informed by groundwork related to doxxing by the researcher (Lee, 2020) and previous research on online aggressive behavior by other researchers (e.g., Assimakopoulos et al., 2017; Baider & Constantinou, 2020). The interpretation of discourse practices was also situated within the broader socio-historical background of Hong Kong to uncover the ideologies that shape the participants' perceptions. The findings from analyses of forum posts and interviews were compared with institutional discourses. The purpose of this comparative analysis is to reveal possible mismatches between young people and the official understanding of doxxing.

To ensure rigor and transparency, the data were coded and repeatedly reviewed by both the author and a full-time research assistant. Regular consultation sessions were also held with trained student assistants, who are also regular users of LIHKG, to interpret context-specific language found on the forum. This collaborative approach helped validate interpretations in the identification of doxxing incidents and discourse patterns. Coding memos were also produced to document major decisions made in the coding, analysis, and interpretation of data. The memos also noted theoretical or conceptual connections that emerged from the data. Patterns of digital practices and discourse strategies, and similarities and differences among social actors (i.e., whether they take up similar or different strategies when representing the same instance of doxxing) were noted. The coding matrix was drafted and constantly reviewed and revised by all members of the project team (see Appendix for the full coding scheme).

3 Language and Discourse Strategies of Doxxing Discussions Online

This section analyzes the language and discourse strategies employed in online discussions of and about doxxing, as well as LIHKG users' reactions to doxxing-related news. The analytical focus is on how forum participants construct, justify, and legitimize the practice. Informed by CDA concepts, this section discusses the interplay of intertextuality, linguistic choices, and legitimation strategies in shaping doxxing practices.

It is important to note that the data analyzed in this Element does not immediately warrant classification as illegal doxxing, nor is it the intention of this Element to determine legal consequences. Rather, the focus is on the ways language and discourse may be manipulated or reframed when forum users attempt to disclose others' personal information. The posts to be examined may contain information about unknown parties, reactions to news related to doxxing and its legal context in Hong Kong, or reposts of news about doxxing incidents.

3.1 Doxxing as Intertextual and Recontextualized Discourse

To illustrate what a doxxing incident may look like on LIHKG, consider a thread with the subject line, *"There's a dog that really wants to be famous. Will you help it or not?!!"* This thread exemplifies the structure and rhetorical strategies often used to expose personal information for public scrutiny. The various components of this post will first be unpacked to reveal how doxxing operates intertextually within the forum's discursive norms. Doing so also helps to contextualize the data discussed in the subsequent sections.

The euphemistic title hints at doxxing behavior. First, the metaphor of a "dog" serves as a derogatory reference to the target – a police officer – a common dehumanizing label used by activists and protesters. The playful and ironic tone downplays the seriousness of the content, which involves disclosing personal information for the purpose of naming and shaming, a common tactic in online shaming and digilantism (Murumaa-Mengel & Muuli, 2021). The post also calls to action, "Will you help it or not?!!," which actively invites participation from other forum users.

The majority of the initial posts in this thread are represented by the most direct and explicit form of intertextuality, or what Fairclough (1992) calls "manifest intertextuality." The post is a lengthy one, comprising nine screenshots taken from a police officer's Facebook profile. The thread comprises three intertextual components:

- Part 1 of the thread includes a screenshot of the officer's photo from his Facebook account, captioned with his full name and family members' names (wife, son) in Chinese, which reads, "Name of dog: [full name of the officer]; Family history of dog: A mother, a wife called [name of wife], a son called [name of son]."
- Part 2 of the post features a collage of the officer's Facebook screenshots and online comment exchanges, including a political debate with a student and a meme mocking the police commissioner.
- Part 3 of the post contains five private photos of the officer's family and friends from Facebook.

3.1.1 Multimodal Intertextuality in Doxxing: Screenshots as Personal History

The post described demonstrates that online doxxing relies heavily on *multimodal intertextuality*, where screenshots, primarily from social media and private communication, act as the primary tool for recontextualizing antecedent texts. As shown, the post is created by making intertextual references to images and texts from the police officer's Facebook feed, which in itself contains additional layers of multimodal texts. The shared material also includes text-based comments from the officer's Facebook friends, embedding heteroglossic voices from multiple actors (Androutsopoulos, 2010). Instead of creating intertextual links through words only, the antecedent texts, whether they are originally images or words, are represented as screenshot images, creating *text-as-image* and *image-as-image* intertextual relations.

In disclosing the police officer's and his family's identities, all three of Douglas' (2016) categories of doxxing are evident. To *de-anonymize*, the full names of the officer, his son, and his wife are revealed in the Facebook screenshots. These names are intertextual both internally to the names captured in the screenshots in this post, and externally to the officer's Facebook site outside the forum, and to their real-world legal identities.

This post also illustrates *targeting doxxing* (Douglas, 2016). Although no information about home address is shared, the screenshots reveal the officer's Facebook account name, and thus anyone can look him up and locate him "virtually" with an online search. Douglas (2016) makes a clear distinction between de-anonymizing and targeting doxxing in that the former reveals a connection between a pseudonym and one's legal identity, while the latter aims to physically locate someone. In this post, the disclosure of the officer's Facebook profile is not only to reveal the officer's real name, but to ensure that he becomes "locatable" at least virtually. When the officer is identified online, abusers are likely to locate his other social media profiles, with the aim of inducing further public scrutiny or cyberbullying. This practice is clearly connected to "call-out" and "cancel" culture, in that netizens rapidly share and reshare targets' personal information for public shaming because of their alleged wrongdoing (Clark, 2020).

3.1.2 Unattributed Intertextuality and Assumption

Delegitimizing is the primary motive behind this post. By sharing screenshots of the officer's social media comments on political topics, his words are recontextualized to frame him as ideologically aligned with the Hong Kong authorities. This act not only exposes the officer's political stance but also invites further scrutiny from forum participants.

Alongside the screenshots, the thread initiator adds the caption:

> *You don't even know how to use Facebook. Stop messing with other people's children*

This requires some unpacking. The pronoun "*you*" establishes a cohesive link to the officer in the image, creating a simulated dialogue between the author and the officer. This remark points to the fact that the officer has made his own Facebook posts public, implying he is responsible for his own exposure. The adverb "*even*" (連 lin4 in Cantonese) presupposes that, as a police officer, he should be more media literate and sensitive to online privacy. There is also an implicit attribution to Facebook's privacy policy, which allows users to control who can view their posts. The second part of the comment implicitly references the police's use of violence against protesters, many of whom are young people, thus framing the officer's actions as "*messing with other people's children.*"

The purpose of this intertextual relation is not to criticize the officer's privacy insensitivity but to condemn him as a police officer supporting the extradition bill, which most forum participants oppose. The negative evaluation of the officer's competence in using Facebook also creates an unattributed intertextual connection to the government's stance on protecting police privacy despite alleged misconduct (SCMP, 2019). This is not intertextuality per se but rather what Fairclough (2003) terms *assumption*, which depends on meanings that are "shared and can be taken as given" (p.55). Although it is unclear if the officer was involved in violent crackdowns, the forum participants' common ground is the assumption that most police officers have "messed with other people's children," thus deserving no respect. These intertextual links and assumptions reinforce the binary opposition between "Us" (activists) and "Them" (police, government) (Oddo, 2011), creating a context where doxxing police officers is legitimized and justified.

3.2 Linguistic Re-Appropriation of Doxxing

This section examines how doxxing-related practices are linguistically reframed by LIHKG users through strategic language use. Drawing on concepts of CDA, the analysis focuses on how forum participants creatively re-appropriate language to construct doxxing as morally acceptable. Three recurring linguistic devices are identified across the dataset – metaphor, euphemism, and irony – which work together to downplay the perceived harm of doxxing.

3.2.1 Dehumanizing Metaphors

In CDA, metaphors are a key linguistic device to convey ideology in discursive legitimation of discriminatory and negative othering discourses (Koller, 2020; Hart, 2021). In the LIHKG forum data, dehumanizing metaphors involving "dog" imagery emerge as a recurring strategy to delegitimize all Hong Kong police officers, regardless of their level of involvement in the protests. The discourse analysis reveals multiple linguistic variants referring to "dogs," including:

- 黑狗 (Black dog)
- 警犬 (Police dog)
- 癲狗 (Rabid dog)
- 警曱/狗官 (Police cockroach/dog official)
- 走狗 (running dog)
- 支那狗 (China dog)
- 魔犬 (demon dog)

These dog metaphors, or any animal metaphors, serve to dehumanize police officers by positioning them "'lower down' in the Great Chain of Being" (Hart, 2021, p. 232). By framing officers as less than human, these metaphors facilitate "soft hate" strategies in online aggression. Dehumanization also enacts what

Bandura et al. (1996) refer to as "moral disengagement" (Bandura et al., 1996). According to Bandura et al., acts of moral disengagement, such as blame attribution, displacement of responsibility, and dehumanization, allow individuals to justify or rationalize harmful or unethical behavior, such as doxxing, thereby disengaging their moral self-sanctions and avoiding feelings of guilt.

3.2.2 Euphemism

The use of euphemism serves as a strategic linguistic device to legitimize or downplay the harmful nature of doxxing. One notable example is the term 老豆搵仔 (or "DadFindBoy" in English, literally "Dad looking for son"), specifically used to refer to deanonymizing of masked or unidentifiable police officers during the protests. The "DadFindBoy" channel, a Telegram group, was used to gather and publish personal information about police officers and their families. The channel's name metaphorically frames the act of doxxing as a familial search, where "dads" (activists) are looking for their lost "sons" (police officers). Despite the arrest of the administrator of the "DadFindBoy" channel on Telegram, the LIHKG participants still continue to use this term when they refer to the doxxing of police. This reframing downplays the severity of doxxing by portraying it as a kind act of reunification rather than a malicious behavior.

A related example is "幫推 順便幫埋黑狗搵仔女" ("Help bump [this thread]. And by the way, let's help the black dog find its kids too."). This comment embeds a disguised call for doxxing within a seemingly harmless request. The term 黑狗 ("black dog") is a derogatory term for police officers, in which "black" evokes a negative association with 黑社會 (black society, a reference to triads or gangsters), implying that the police are as morally corrupted as criminals. Framing doxxing as an act of helping a dog reunite with its offspring, doxxing is recast as a service rather than an abusive act of privacy invasion. The casual tone ("by the way") further trivializes the severity of the doxxing, presenting it as a secondary, almost incidental, activity. Another common protest-related euphemistic expression is 發夢 ("dreaming"), which was used as a euphemism for attending or recounting experiences at the protests (Leung, 2019). Protesters would say they "dreamed" they were at a protest site and discuss their experiences without having to directly admit involvement in potentially illegal activities. For example, a commenter wrote, "發夢夢見 開槍 黑警" ("In my dream, I saw a black cop shooting"). This allows the user to share their first-hand experience at the protest sites without explicitly saying that they actually saw the shooting.

As can be seen, these euphemistic expressions are also metaphorical, which can be referred to as metaphorical euphemism. In political discourse, metaphorical euphemism serves to soften controversial issues and frame them positively (Crespo-Fernández, 2018). Similarly, in doxxing-related discussions on LIHKG, euphemisms such as dreaming help obscure the potentially malicious intent and harmful consequences of doxxing practices.

3.2.3 Irony

According to Fairclough (2003), irony is intertextual because it means "saying one thing but meaning another" that "echoes someone else's utterance" (p. 123). Irony in doxxing discussions serves multiple functions. For one thing, it allows users to challenge and subvert dominant narratives in a covert manner. Such covertness becomes a protective mechanism as it conveys resistance without overtly challenging authorities and legal boundaries. In the LIHKG forum data, being doxxed is ironically framed as an "honor," as illustrated in the following examples:

(1)   黑警係正義嘅
      所以要公開表揚佢哋大家

      ("Black cops are righteous; Therefore, we should publicly commend them, everyone.")

(2)   公開表揚愛港愛國既警務人員都有錯?

      ("What's wrong with publicly commending patriotic police officers who love Hong Kong?")

(3)   Good job 請繼續宣揚警隊英勇事跡

      ("Good job, please continue to promote the police force's heroic deeds.")

Examples (1) to (3) carry a seemingly positive undertone, using verbs of praise such as 表揚 (commend/praise) and 宣揚 (promote/propagate). However, the intent of these comments is expected to be interpreted through the audience's awareness of the context of communication. The immediate context of the discussion threads, that is, posts reacting to the newly introduced doxxing law, coupled with the broader social context of escalating conflicts between protesters and the police, makes it clear that the police are meant to be condemned, not praised. The meanings of these comments are uncovered within a frame consistent with the forum participants' negative stance toward the police. The writers of these posts assume that their audience will recognize "praising" as an ironic reference to doxxing. The ironic effect is created through the exact opposite of what is said is what is meant (Assimakopoulos et al., 2017). Here, "praising" or "promoting" an officer is a coded reference to the act of doxxing, that is, publicly revealing personal information as a form of social sanction. The irony is thus constructed through the deliberate reversal of meaning: what is said as praise is meant as condemnation.

3.3 Legitimation Discourse Strategies

Legitimation strategies, as theorized within CDA, aim to address the fundamental questions of "Why should we do this?" or "Why should we do this in this way?" (Van Leeuwen, 2007). There are four primary conceptual categories in Van Leeuwen's (2007) legitimation framework: *authorization* (reference to authority), *moral evaluation* (reference to value systems), *rationalization* (reference to goals and uses), and *mythopoesis* (legitimation through storytelling). These strategies operate through complex discursive manipulations in order to transform potentially controversial topics or actions into socially acceptable practices. When discursively framing the doxxing of police officers on LIHKG, participants provide arguments to answer "Why do we doxx?" or "Why is doxxing the right thing to do?"

3.3.1 Rationalization: Doxxing as Self-Defense

Rationalization is one of the most explicit forms of legitimation (Fairclough, 2003). When rationalizing an action, reasons for the action are given based on principles of right or wrong, or norm conformity (Van Leeuwen, 2007). Objective moral evaluation of actors is also given to justify one's controversial action (Oddo, 2011). Legitimizing doxxing through rationalization is also achieved through stating the purpose and purposiveness of the action in order to answer the question, "Why is disclosing someone else's personal data morally right and effective?" Rationalization discourse explains an action by reference to "goals and uses" (Van Leeuwen, 2007). The aim of rationalizing an action is to frame it as a sensible decision, as "the right thing to do."

Specific to the LIHKG data, the rationalization strategy answers the question of "What is the purpose of doxxing the police?" Commenters provide rational reasons to explain doxxing as serving real purposes, as illustrated in examples (4) and (5):

(4)   你搞人地個仔
        人地咪搞返你個仔囉

        ("You mess with someone else's son. That's why they mess with your son in return.")

(5)   如果你係真心問
        我會答你因為除左呢個方法外

能制裁警察既手段近乎冇
所以大家都唔反對呢種做法

> ("If you're genuinely asking me, I'd say that apart from this method (doxxing), there are almost no means to sanction the police, so none of us opposes this approach.")

In both examples, doxxing is rationalized in the name of a form of reciprocity, self-defense, and as the only approach to achieve justice. Example (4) is a reactive comment to a British police officer's family being doxxed, including the school his children attended, leading to physical abuse and bullying at the school. The commenter rationalizes doxxing as an "equal" response to what police have done to others' children during the protests. It directly presents doxxing as justified retaliation ("mess with your son in return"). The implied logic here is that if the police have done wrong to the young protesters (who are also others' children), it is acceptable for their supporters to respond in kind. This rationalization seeks to legitimize doxxing by framing it as reciprocal justice.

Example (5) rationalizes doxxing by scrutinizing the power imbalance between civilians and the police. To the activists, the police are unprofessional, biased, and possess excessive power, and there is no way for the public to challenge their authority. By emphasizing this power imbalance, the commenter conveys a sense of helplessness, thus justifying the use of unconventional tactics such as doxxing as the only way to achieve justice. By stating that there are "almost no means to sanction the police," this example positions doxxing as a last resort where civilians can exercise their agency. The statement that "none of us opposes" doxxing suggests the collective sentiments among activists and supporters that doxxing is a necessary tool.

3.3.2 (Re)definition: Neutralizing Doxxing

(Re-)definition is a "theoretical legitimation" strategy where actions are legitimized not in terms of purposes and effectiveness, but through defining an action in terms of "another, moralized activity" (Van Leeuwen, 2007, p. 103). Van Leeuwen originally categorizes definition as a form of rationalization. However, in the context of LIHKG, (re-)defining doxxing is a salient practice that deserves its own category. For one thing, facing the possibility of their controversial posts being removed by authorities, it is important for the forum participants to develop a shared interpretation of what doxxing is or, more importantly, what it is not.

(6) 其實所謂起底都係將啲差佬自己喺社交平台 post 出嚟嘅資料 share 上嚟啫 咁都犯法

("Actually, so-called doxxing is just sharing information that the cops themselves posted on social media. How is that illegal?")

(7) 政治既思維係特別 D
連登既所謂起底
只係將放係 public domain 既資料整理

("Political thinking is different. LIHKG's so-called doxxing is just organizing information already in the public domain.")

Examples (6) and (7) redefine doxxing as the redistribution of publicly available data, which downplays its malicious nature. In the LIHKG data, doxxing is often prefixed with 所謂 ("so-called"), which signals the writers' distancing from the negative connotations of the word. A common argumentation strategy in the data is to claim that the exposed information is already made public by the targets, which serves to neutralize doxxing as morally acceptable (characterizing it as "sharing information," "organizing information"), rather than as a violation of privacy.

Once redefined and neutralized as mere information sharing, the commenters proceed to delegitimize the doxxing law, suggesting that it is too stringent. The rhetorical question 咁都犯法 ("How is that illegal?") in Example (6) marks the commenter's epistemic stance and skepticism toward the ambiguous legal definition of doxxing. Stylistically, rhetorical questions are a powerful linguistic device to focus "on the argument in the message, thereby enhancing the goal, which is persuasion" (Ademilokun & Taiwo, 2013, p. 447). In this case, the writer employs a rhetorical question to persuade other forum participants that doxxing is not illegal. Rhetorical questions are often juxtaposed with an implicit intertextual reference to external voices – in this case, to the legal discourse that criminalizes doxxing behavior, allowing the writer to indirectly challenge the authority of the law.

Example (7) further contrasts "political thinking" (政治既思維) with what the commenter sees as overly narrow legal definitions of doxxing. This juxtaposition foregrounds a perceived mismatch between lay and official interpretations of legal terms. Such redefinition creates a shared interpretive framework within the forum community, which enables participants to collectively justify their actions within the broader attempts to detach doxxing from its harmful intent.

Some participants *normalize* doxxing by defining it as "the way things are" (Van Leeuwen, 2007). Normalization is a discourse strategy that frames ideologies and social practices as normal and commonplace, thus attributing what would have been unacceptable behavior a more neutral quality (see Rheindorf, 2019). In the case of legitimizing doxxing, expressions such as "many," "inevitable" are often used to frame doxxing as commonplace, thus not requiring legal attention.

(8) 不是網民的專利, 很多機構 (包括政府機構如秘密警察) 都可起底

("It's not something exclusive to internet users; many organizations (including government agencies like secret police) can also doxx people.")

(9) 在資訊科技過於發達的環境下, 這件事很難避免

("In a world where information technology is overly advanced, this kind of thing (doxxing) is inevitable.")

Examples (8) and (9) legitimize doxxing as a common and inevitable outcome of technological advancement. Example (8) describes doxxing as "不是網民的專利" ("not something exclusive to internet users") and a common practice by "很多機構" ("many organizations"). By stating that doxxing is not unique to online communities but is also engaged in by institutions, the act of doxxing is given a high degree of authority and legitimacy. Using examples of government agencies like the secret police, again, serves to detach doxxing from its malicious intent, implying that if government institutions can do it, then it must be acceptable for civilians to follow suit.

Example (9) frames doxxing as a natural byproduct of technological advancement. By presenting doxxing as inevitable (很難避免) in the digital age, the commenter shifts focus away from individual responsibility to broader social changes. Similar to the function of Example (8), this comment serves to reduce the severity of doxxing, framing it as an ordinary part of life rather than a deliberate invasion of privacy. The strategies identified here also parallel Sykes and Matza's (1957) "techniques of neutralization" in their analysis of juvenile delinquency, where individuals use specific rhetorical devices to temporarily override moral constraints that would normally prevent illegitimate behavior.

3.3.3 Negative-Other Construction: Degrading Authorities

By attributing negative qualities to the out-group, actors are able to construct a "negative-Other" representation, thus positioning themselves as morally superior or "in the right." Such negative constructions are often linguistically realized by attaching negative labels to the out-group, or through negative moral evaluation of them (Wodak, 2001). Common linguistic strategies include dehumanizing the "out-group" and attacking the out-group's intelligence or competence, and so on. In the LIHKG forum data, the police and the government are often represented in negative terms. This serves to unify forum users by establishing a shared target and reinforcing in-group solidarity.

There are several ways through which forum participants attribute negative qualities to police officers to legitimize doxxing. First, the out-group (i.e., the police) is linguistically realized by *nomination* strategy, that is, the use of membership categorization devices to define out-groups (Wodak, 2001), such as dehumanizing the police as 垃圾 ("trash") and 警犬 ("police dog") in example (10). Second, "police" (警) is often premodified by "black" (黑), which means gangsters in Cantonese (Choy, 2020). The colloquial expression has been frequently used since July 2019, when the police allegedly colluded with gangsters to attack protesters in a metro station. 毅進警犬 ("Yijin police dogs") in example (10) not only dehumanizes the police, but also mocks their educational background by referencing the Yijin (毅進) diploma programme for underachieving students who are not eligible for university admission, implying they are uneducated or illiterate. Example (11) even further frames Yijin as a syndrome, implying that police officers who are suffering from it as intelligence-deficient. It is reported that many police officers graduated from that programme.[6] The activists, the majority of whom are university students, were calling the police "毅進仔" ("Yijin guys") to delegitimize their professionalism.

(10)   社會垃圾 毅進警犬 賣港惡賊

   ("Social trash, Yijin police dogs, traitors who sell out Hong Kong.")

(11)   毅氏綜合症呀! 毅進仔! IQ高唔高過 50 呀?

   ("Yijin syndrome! Yijin boy! Is your IQ not higher than 50?")

By mocking the police's intelligence, labeling them as "social trash," and implying their low IQ, these constructions position the police, that is, law enforcement, as inferior and illegitimate, thereby justifying doxxing as a form of moral rectification.

Lexical choices in examples (12) and (13), such as "lawless," "oppression," "bandit," and "murderer," help foreground the police's use of excessive violence, thus holding them accountable and framing them as deserving to be doxxed.

(12)   無天無法, 專責打壓
   濫用私刑, 猶在賊營

   ("Lawless, specializing in oppression, abusing private punishment, still in the bandit camp")

---

[6] *Apple Daily*, 四成半新聘警員毅進畢業 ("45% of newly employed police graduated from Yijin") https://hk.appledaily.com/local/20200408/E2D7PI3NDNBFXNO5C6CQMJYXX4/.

(13)   殺人兇手 警員 xxx [name of officer]

("Murderer, Police Officer [name]")

Example (12) is also noteworthy in that it employs a poetic style resembling traditional Chinese couplets. The use of four four-character lines with rhymes creates a poetic effect, which adds to the rhetorical power of the negative-Other representation. In contrast, example (13) is more direct and confrontational. By labeling a specific officer as a "murderer," this comment explicitly accuses the police of extreme violence, positioning them as immoral and deserving of doxxing.

The targeted out-group in the data includes not only the police, but also government officials involved in implementing the doxxing law, notably the Privacy Commissioner, who demanded more authority "to order the relevant social platforms or websites to remove or stop uploading content and posts that involved doxxing" (SCMP, 2019). Reacting to this news report, one forum user wrote:

(14)   私隱專員, 掹大隻眼睇清楚喇!
全部係X生自己 post 上 facebook 㗎!
全部係佢自己 set public 㗎!唔該你地派人去教人班毅進仔點用 facebook 先啦!

("Privacy Commissioner, open your eyes and see clearly! Everything on Facebook was posted by Mr. X himself! He made everything public himself! Please send someone to teach those Yijin boys how to use Facebook first!")

Example (14) delegitimizes the Privacy Commissioner through multiple means. First, his professional judgment and credibility are being challenged. The imperative and directive speech act 掹大隻眼睇清楚 ("Open your eyes and see clearly") is a Cantonese colloquial expression, implying that he has been negligent or mistaken in his assessment of doxxing cases. Second, through implicit redefinitions of "public" and "private," the commenter legitimizes doxxing by holding the targeted officer accountable – 全部係佢自己 set public 㗎 "He made everything public himself") – emphasizing that the information was willingly shared by the target on a public platform. By focusing on the target's own action, the commenter suggests that the Privacy Commissioner is misinterpreting the situation by equating re-sharing something on public Facebook pages with doxxing.

Blame shifting is also at play in Example (14). Blame shifting or blame avoidance, as a discourse strategy, involves redirecting or shifting responsibility for negative outcomes from oneself or one's group to another individual or group. This strategy is commonly used in political communication to evade accountability and protect one's reputation. For example, politicians may employ blame shifting by presenting others, such as opposing parties as accountable for societal issues or crises (Hansson & Page, 2024). In the LIHKG forum data, blame shifting often occurs as counter-discourse, when forum participants redirect the responsibility to doxxed targets as the ones who first disclosed their own personal information online. The commenter in (14) shifts the blame to the police as he made his Facebook public, and away from those actually sharing the information and shaming the target.

When responsibilities are shifted to the targets, their "victim" status has also been undermined. Discourse can be used to construct and contest victim identities. In examples (15) to (17), the commenters are actively working to undermine the victim status of the doxxed individuals by highlighting their own agency (e.g., carelessness) in making the information public.

(15)   自己放上網怨得邊個

    ("Who is to blame when you post it online yourself"?)

(16)   邊個逼你放個人資料上社交媒體

    ("No one forces you to post personal information on social media.")

(17)   起底無問題, 只係上網唔小心

    ("Doxxing isn't the issue, it's just people being careless online.")

In short, this subsection has examined how LIHKG forum participants construct a negative-Other representation of authorities, primarily the police and government officials, to legitimize doxxing practices. This is achieved through various discursive strategies, including dehumanization and blame shifting through the language of negative evaluation. These strategies delegitimize authorities as incompetent both personally and professionally, thus framing them as deserving and valid targets of doxxing and public shaming. The victimhood of the police as doxxed targets has also been challenged. These discourses together become yet another coping mechanism to create a discursive environment where doxxing is seen as a justifiable or even unavoidable consequence of using social media, rather than a deliberate act of harm.

3.3.4 Victimizing "US": Doxxers Are Powerless

As well as negative evaluation of the out-group, actors engaged in doxxing discourse may simultaneously draw on constructive strategies (Van Leeuwen & Wodak, 1999) to seek solidarity. Some of these strategies involve categorizing the in-group as victims of the out-group's immoral actions (Oddo, 2011). This victimization strategy is a powerful tool for legitimizing otherwise controversial practices such as doxxing. By positioning themselves as powerless or wronged, forum participants create a moral framework in which doxxing practices are justified as defensive or proportional responses rather than aggression.

Examples (18) and (19) are responses to a news article reporting doxxed police officers feeling 委屈 "wronged" after their families being doxxed.

(18) 打人射人唔見你話委屈？十幾個圍一個學生唔見你委屈？人地父母啲仔女比你地打到仆街都未出聲

("You beat and shoot people, yet you never said you were wronged.[7] Ten or more (police officers) surrounding one student, yet you didn't say you were wronged? Others' children are beaten badly by you, and their parents haven't even spoken up")

(19) 我哋俾你哋屈做暴徒都好撚委屈

("We are so fucking wronged to be framed as rioters by you")

These two examples employ the evaluation strategy of "comparison" (Van Leeuwen, 2007). In (18), the speaker contrasts the powerful, allegedly violent police with the powerless injured protesters, foregrounding the asymmetry of suffering and implying that the police's sense of grievance is misplaced or hypocritical. The rhetorical questions serve to amplify the protesters' victim status and delegitimize the police's complaints of their families suffering from being doxxed. Example (19) shifts the focus to the emotional impact of protesters being collectively labeled "rioters," using intensifying language ("so fucking wronged") to convey a sense of deep injustice and collective emotion. These emotionally charged discourses of victimhood allow the commenters to construct a power imbalance between authorities and the protesters, that is, police as oppressive and protesters as vulnerable, thus also legitimizing doxxing as a proportionate response. Framing protesters as powerless also helps strengthen the collective identity of the doxxing community within and beyond the forum.

3.4 Legitimation and the Moral Economy of Doxxing

In summary, this section has shown that the legitimation of doxxing is achieved through a complex interplay of linguistic and discursive strategies, including dehumanization metaphors, irony, euphemism, rationalization, (re)definition, negative-other construction, and victimization. Table 1 and Table 2 summarize

---

[7] Here, 委屈 (to feel wronged/treated unfairly) is being used ironically: The commenter contrasts police violence against students and civilians with the police now claiming to be victims of doxxing. The counter-discourse lies in rejecting the police's claim to being "wronged," by pointing out that victims of police violence did not receive the same level of sympathy from the government.

Table 1 Linguistic and discourse strategies that legitimize doxxing on LIHKG

Strategy	Linguistic feature	Example	Discourse function
Rationalization	Purpose clauses (e.g., 為咗 due to …), conditionals (如果 If … 就 then …), causal conjunctions (因為 Because, 所以 So)	如果你係真心問，我會答你因為除咗呢個方法外，能制裁警察既手段既近乎冇，所以大家都唔反對呢種做法。 ("If you're really asking me, I'd say that apart from this method, there are almost no means to sanction the police, so none of us opposes this approach.")	Self-defense
Euphemism	Metaphorical substitutions (e.g., 老豆搵仔 DadFindBoys)	幫推，順便幫埋黑狗搵仔女。 ("Help bump [this thread]. And by the way, let's help the black dog find its kids too.")	Downplaying/obscuring illegality
Dehumanizing metaphor	Animal metaphors (e.g., 警犬 police dog)	警犬、癲狗 (Black dog, police dog, rabid dog)	Moral disengagement, delegitimizing out-group
Irony	Semantic reversal (using praise to mean blame), context-dependent implicature, hyperbolic modifiers	公開表揚愛港愛國既警務人員都有錯? (What's wrong with publicly commending patriotic police officers who love Hong Kong?)	Covert resistance
(Re)definition	Hedging (所謂 so-called), rhetorical questions	其實所謂起底都係將差佬自己喺社交平台post出嚟嘅資料 share 上嚟咋，咁都犯法? (Actually, so-called doxxing is just sharing information that the cops themselves posted on social media. How is that illegal?)	Normalization, redefining boundaries

Table 2 Linguistic and discourse strategies that legitimize doxxing on LIHKG

Strategy	Linguistic feature	Example	Discourse function
Negative-Other Construction	Nomination/name-calling (metaphors)	社會垃圾、毅進警犬、賣港惡賊 Social trash, Yijin police dogs, traitors who sell out Hong Kong.	Delegitimization of out-group, in-group reinforcement
Victimization	emotive intensifiers (好撚委屈 so fucking wronged), pronouns, inclusive first-person plurals (我哋 we)	我哋俾你哋屈做暴徒都好撚委屈 (We are so fucking wronged to be framed as rioters by you)	Solidarity building
Blame Shifting	rhetorical questions (邊個逼你 Who forced you to …?),	自己放上網怨得邊個? (Who is to blame when you post it online yourself?)	Accountability avoidance, shifting responsibility

the linguistic and discursive strategies employed by LIHKG users in the data to legitimize doxxing and related practices.

The analysis of legitimation clearly demonstrates the discursive nature of doxxing, rather than treating it as just a behavioral issue. As argued throughout the Element, language and discourse play a central role in shaping what counts as doxxing and why it is the way it is. LIHKG users often rely on linguistic features such as metaphors, rhetorical questions, and irony to rationalize or redefine doxxing practices. From a critical perspective, these linguistic choices are not random; rather, they are strategically deployed by social actors to serve wider discourse functions, such as moral disengagement, subversion, and self-defense. These legitimization and discourse processes are best understood through the lens of what Thompson (1971) refers to as the "moral economy," which describes a legitimizing notion that informs crowd actions that are based on defending perceived rights or customs supported by a wider consensus of the community. By drawing on a shared set of linguistic and discourse processes that legitimize doxxing, LIHKG users collectively negotiate the moral norms of online practices. It is worth noting that these strategies are not mutually exclusive but are often used in combination. For example, in the data, the strategy of (re)definition often co-occurs with blame shifting, whereas dehumanization is evident in almost all cases of negative-Other construction.

The analysis of legitimation discourse also sheds light on understanding the limitations of legal frameworks to regulate digital behaviors such as doxxing. As the discussion in this section reveals, online users can skillfully and strategically manipulate their language to downplay and legitimize what might be controversial practices. In legislation, it is important to address the subtle yet recurring discursive processes in digital communication that often lead to the perpetuation of online harm.

4 Attitudes and Perceptions Toward Doxxing

While the previous section examines the linguistic devices and discursive strategies that LIHKG users deploy to legitimize doxxing in their online comments, it is equally important to consider how such discourses are perceived and interpreted by the general public. This section explores the attitudes and perceptions of the university student participants in the project, drawing primarily on interview data. Understanding attitudes offers important insights into the ways in which social norms and ethical boundaries are negotiated in people's everyday lives. People's exposure to everyday online discourse, such as reading or writing posts on LIHKG, plays a crucial role in shaping how they approach controversial behaviors online (Barton & Lee, 2013/2025); their attitudes in turn inform and sustain the everyday practices of doxxing. As Fairclough (1992, p. 64) notes, "discourse contributes to the construction of systems of knowledge and belief." This section, therefore, moves beyond analysis of forum posts to examine the values and beliefs that underpin how doxxing is interpreted by the lay public.

4.1 A Spectrum of Attitudes

The interview data reveal the multifaceted attitudes toward doxxing among university students in Hong Kong, who constitute the core group of LIHKG users. The findings show how discourse actively shapes users' ethical norms, legitimizes digilantism, and negotiates power dynamics in online spaces. A central theme in the interviews is the pervasive discourse of ambivalence surrounding doxxing, which often emerges from a perceived failure of the legal system to uphold justice or ensure accountability. The examples come from both focus group and in-depth individual interviews with participants who are either active LIHKG users, bystanders, or those who had first-hand experience of doxxing incidents, as well as from respondents' open-ended comments in the online survey. Attitudes toward doxxing in Hong Kong span a complex spectrum ranging from positive evaluation to normalization, conditional acceptance, and even disapproval.

4.1.1 Positive Evaluation: Altruism and Justice-Seeking

At one end of the attitudinal spectrum, doxxing is frequently framed by participants as a morally justified act linked with *public interest* and the pursuit of *justice*. This view reflects broader online practices in Hong Kong in recent years, where it is not uncommon for people to engage in public shaming by exposing the personal data of perceived wrongdoers. Common targets of online public shaming in Hong Kong range from reckless drivers to scammers, sexual harassment offenders, to the so-called 渣男, a Cantonese colloquial term referring to men who behave irresponsibly or immorally in romantic relationships (loosely translated as "scumbag" or "toxic man") (see HKFP, 2023; SCMP, 2023). In these instances, netizens often frame public shaming and doxxing not as an immoral or illegal behavior, but as an act of civic responsibility or public service.

This background helps to contextualize the attitude-related findings of this study, which identify a significant portion of participants positively describing doxxing under the name of altruism or the pursuit of justice.

In the LIHKG data, bystander commenters often employ the verb 推 ("push"), a forum slang meaning to promote a post for visibility, as in: 推 下等多d人知 ("push, so more people will know"), to endorse the spreading of doxxed information for the public good. This perception of doxxing echoes Anderson and Wood's (2021, p. 209) definition of "public interesting doxxing," which is:

> motivated by a belief that the release of personally identifiable or proprietary information will promote the welfare or well-being of the general public … Public interest doxxing may take numerous forms, including as a mechanism for holding governments, institutions, and public figures accountable, as well as a mechanism for issuing public safety announcements through, for example, releasing personally identifiable information about predatory Tinder dates.

Participants in both focus group and individual interviews similarly expressed support for public interest doxxing, as stated by Respondent R:

> *Respondent R*: 你公眾利益去起底呢, 我覺得完全冇問題, totally fine, 係 justified, 而政府亦都唔應該去立法禁止。
>
> ("If it's for public interest, I think there's absolutely no problem at all. It's totally fine, it's justified. And the government shouldn't legislate against it.")

Respondent R expresses a positive moral evaluation of doxxing, using emphatic adverbials "完全" ("totally") to stress its legitimacy. The opposition to government legislation reveals the respondent's counter-hegemonic stance: the participant sees legal efforts to criminalize all doxxing as unjustified and even harmful to public interest.

Taken together, the interview participants viewed doxxing as serving three key functions:

(i) Upholding Social Justice and Fostering Moral Behavior

The expression 伸張正義 ("to uphold justice") was repeatedly used by interviewees to characterize the motivation behind doxxing. The idea of "justice" here seems to diverge from formal legal definitions and instead aligns with a kind of informal, community-based moral norm. Interviewees described situations where doxxing was seen as justified despite the target's actions not being illegal. For example, videos capturing rude behavior in customer service settings are often posted on social media for public shaming. This echoes Garcés-Conejos Blitvich's (2022) observation that online shaming can be perceived as fostering cooperative and moral behavior in society.

Respondent K: 動機係良性嘅, 即係所謂係想警惡懲奸, 伸張正義啦, 我覺得係好嘅件事。

("The motive is well-meaning, i.e. to 'warn the wicked and punish the treacherous' and uphold justice. I think it's a good thing.")

When asked to comment on a known case of doxxing a sexual harassment offender, Respondent K draws on a common Chinese idiom 警惡懲奸 ("warn the wicked and punish the treacherous"), which references a long-standing discursive tradition of moral justice in Chinese society. This expression originates in classical Chinese and Chinese heroic literature, where justice is often enacted not through legal means but through morally righteous individuals (similar to "superheroes") who take action to uphold social order and punish wrongdoers. The use of such culturally embedded idioms aligns with what Wodak (2007) describes as discursive histories, where familiar historical or cultural narratives are used to make contemporary actions feel morally justified and socially acceptable. Here, Respondent K justifies doxxing not only by its outcomes, but also by the intentions of doxxing (動機係良性嘅, "The motive is well-meaning").

Respondent R: 有時候睇到連登嘅起底情況, 之後佢哋可能覺得嗰個人唔好, 想用另類嘅方式去伸張正義, 所以先至去做呢一個起底嘅事情。

("Sometimes when I see doxxing incidents on LIHKG, maybe they [doxxers] think that the person involved was bad and they want to pursue justice in an alternative way – so they resort to doxxing.")

Respondent R expresses a broader perception of wrongdoing ("the person involved was bad"), with doxxing framed as an "alternative" (另類) form of justice. This reflects the logic of digilantism, where doxxing emerges in online communities as a bottom-up punishment when there is an institutional failure or general distrust in legal systems (Galleguillos, 2022). By positioning doxxing outside formal justice, Respondent R simultaneously expresses disapproval of the formal legal system and endorses informal grassroots "do-it-yourself" action. These discourses of justice align with van Dijk's (1998) *ideological square*, where "our" actions (as digilantes) are legitimized while "their" behavior (as wrongdoers) is delegitimized. The ideological framing positions online actors as defenders of social justice and downplays any potential harm caused to the doxxed targets.

(ii) Doxxing as Deterrent and Public Warning

A second justified purpose of doxxing is its deterrent effect. Several participants believed that exposing a wrongdoer's personal information could help prevent similar behavior by others, thus serving a broader community function. Part of our data-prompted interview included alleged cases of doxxing, and we asked interviewees to comment on a case involving the doxxing of a reckless driver, to which Respondent M said:

> *Respondent M*: 咁嗰個網民可能淨係想叫人哋小心啲嗰個人，叫啲人唔好approach呢個人，咁我哋淨係base on啲咁少嘅資料，咁呢個人可能都淨係想伸張正義姐，叫啲人小心啲啫。
>
> ("Maybe they just want to warn others to be careful, and not to approach this person . . . based on so little information; it's not meant to harm the person but to alert people with information.")

Respondent M suggests that the doxxer may "淨係想叫人哋小心啲嗰個人" ("just want to warn others to be cautious of that person") and "唔好 approach 呢個人" ("not to approach this person"). Here, doxxing is portrayed as a preventive warning system, driven by a desire to inform and protect others from potential harm. Respondent F expands on this preventive logic:

> *Respondent F*: 例如可能我見過畀人性騷擾嘅人公開咗少少嗰個性騷擾這個資料，咁可能係呢啲情況下嗰個想公開佢個人資料嘅人唔係特登意圖令佢有傷害，即係佢唔係特登想佢受傷害嘅，係用啲資訊警惕人，講番件事出嚟，即係類似尋求番個公義咁樣
>
> ("For example, I might have seen someone who was sexually harassed disclose some information about the harasser. In such situations, the person who wants to disclose their personal information might not intentionally mean to cause them harm; they don't intentionally want them to suffer harm, but rather use the information to warn people, to tell the story, which is like seeking justice.")

Respondent F begins the justification of doxxing by citing a clearly morally unacceptable case, sexual harassment, as a context where disclosure of personal information becomes proportionally acceptable, serving to "warn others" and "tell the story." Through repeated emphasis on the absence of malicious intent, "唔係特登想佢受傷害" ("not intentionally meant to cause them harm"), Respondent F discursively shifts the moral evaluation from privacy invasion to its protective motive. The phrase "用啲資訊警惕人" ("use the information to warn people") constructs doxxing as a tool for digilantism, where private information can be transformed into socially meaningful knowledge.

Rather than focusing on negative outcomes, the discourses of both Respondents M and F emphasize the positive value of public disclosure of wrongdoers' information. They both frame doxxing as a deterrent and shift the moral evaluation of doxxing from the harm it may cause to a form of care for society. Again, this reframing positions doxxing as a form of digital safeguarding in contexts where formal legal responses may be inadequate.

(iii) Assisting Formal Investigation

Some interviewees also believed that the information exposed through doxxing could become "evidence" in formal investigations, as illustrated by the following quotes.

Respondent S: 正正係因為啲網民起咗底, 令到佢可以變成一個證據去用司法嘅方式, 可以用虐貓呢一條罪行嚟鋤嗰個虐貓者

"It is precisely because netizens doxxed him that it became possible to use it as evidence in a legal process, like using the offence of animal cruelty to go after the person who abused the cat."

Respondent C: 譬如果有啲人話起佢底啦, 要搵一啲證據去告佢咁樣, 我覺得呢啲都 ok 嘅

"For example, if someone doxxes another person to collect evidence to sue them, I think that's okay"

For Respondents S and C, the value of doxxing lies in its evidentiary function, believing that materials posted online can be considered seriously by formal institutions in the legal process. For example, Respondent C describes how posting a video of someone abusing a cat could potentially result in the perpetrator being charged with animal cruelty. This logic echoes the function of the Human Flesh Search Engine in Mainland China, where crowd-sourced investigations are used to hold wrongdoers accountable (Cheong & Gong, 2010; Gao, 2016; Garcés-Conejos Blitvich, 2022). Within this framing, even if harm is caused, it is seen as a by-product of justice, with doxxing positioned as a necessary step in initiating legal accountability.

Together, when discussing these key functions of doxxing, the interviewees positively reframe doxxing as acceptable and even beneficial to society. Their positive stances are based primarily on intent and the perceived social value of data disclosure. Their words also demonstrate a strong tension between institutional discourses of doxxing and lay moral reasoning, a topic that will be further pursued in Section 5.

4.1.2 Conditional Acceptance: Addressing Institutional Limitations

Many interviewees expressed conditional acceptance of doxxing, that is, doxxing is acceptable or even necessary under specific circumstances, particularly when conventional systems of justice are perceived to have failed. In such cases, doxxing is often justified as a proportional response to perceived ineffective and untrustworthy institutional systems. This perspective is exemplified in the following statements by Respondents K and S:

Respondent K: 有時有啲法律做唔到嘅，我哋就要透過社會輿論去所謂制裁佢...

("Sometimes there're things that the law can't achieve; we must use public opinion to sanction them...")

Respondent S: 當我哋唔太信任或者覺得執法機構未必真係做緊嘅我哋同市民覺得係要做嘅嘢嘅時候，咁好多人就會有呢一個觀緊話呢啲人都唔做嘢囉，不如就由自己做起喇咁樣。

("When we don't quite trust, or feel that law enforcement agencies might not really be doing the things that we and the public think ought to be done, then many people will have this view that, since these people [i.e. the authorities] aren't doing their job, we might as well take it into our own hands and start doing it ourselves.")

These opinions reflect a perceived failure in institutional authority, leading netizens to turn to doxxing as a form of informal justice. The appeal to "public opinion" (社會輿論) suggests that without such alternative methods, broader social harm would persist. The repetition of the inclusive first-person plural pronoun 我哋 ("we") in both quotes constructs an in-group "us" (as opposed to authorities as the out-group "them"), conveying a shared sense of civic responsibility and justifying doxxing as a form of collective action.

Respondent S: 如果佢為咗啲 public interest 或者去行使佢嘅第四權去做一啲嘢嘅話，我自己諗嘅就係我解嘅起底未必一定係罪行。

("If they do something for the public interest or to exercise their fourth estate, then in my view, doxxing is not necessarily a crime.")

Here, Respondent S mobilizes the metaphor of the "fourth estate" to compare doxxing to practices of information disclosure in journalism, so as to reframe doxxing as a form of citizen or investigative reporting. This exemplifies what Van Leeuwen (2007) calls *authorization legitimation*, where referencing socially valued roles, such as journalists, serves to justify an action morally. The hedge "not necessarily a crime" signals discursive negotiation, where the respondent implies that legal definitions of doxxing are not fixed but open to interpretation based on intent and context.

4.1.3 Normalization: Neutralizing Harm through Discursive Framing

Some participants explicitly normalize doxxing by adopting language that serves to neutralize doxxing as a common or even inevitable phenomenon. When normalizing doxxing, these respondents strategically downplay its severity by scrutinizing the term doxxing or offering their own definitions of it. This process aligns with the (re)definition strategy of legitimation by LIHKG users discussed in Section 3.3.2, in which harmful actions are reappropriated in less legally charged terms. By lexicalizing doxxing as a "very neutral term" (好中性嘅詞語), Respondent K, de-emphasizes the negative connotations of doxxing and repositions it as an ordinary, even routine, action on LIHKG.

> *Respondent K:* 我自己本身都覺得起底係一個好中性嘅詞語, 佢唔係帶有負面嘅嘢 ... 對於起底係咪一樣好negative嘅嘢, 我又好保留。
>
> ("I think doxxing is a very neutral term, it doesn't carry negative connotations. ... as for whether doxxing is a very negative thing, I have reservations.")

Calling doxxing a *"neutral term"* demonstrates Respondent K's deliberate discursive effort to lower the moral threshold for doxxing and her approval of doxxing practices. This provides a context for her explicit stance marking at the end of the quote, that is, doxxing is not necessarily negative. Other participants echo this neutral framing by asserting boundaries between acceptable and unacceptable acts:

> *Respondent J:* 即係純粹就咁放條片上網, 我覺得唔係構成起底, 或者係叫做 reasonable 同埋合理。
>
> ("Just posting a video online—I don't think that counts as doxxing; I'd consider it reasonable (and '合理,' 'reasonable' in Chinese.")

Here, Respondent J draws a boundary between what he considers as normal, everyday online activity and the legal definition of doxxing. The phrase "just posting a video" functions as a rhetorical minimizer to de-emphasize the severity of doxxing. By aligning such actions with terms like "reasonable," Respondent J linguistically neutralizes the potential harm of data disclosure and positions it as an acceptable online behavior. This aligns with the broader pattern in the findings in which doxxing is downplayed or legitimized as contextually appropriate based on intent. Another participant links this to contemporary technological changes:

> *Respondent F:* 我覺得尤其是係互聯網咁發達嘅情況底下, 好多嘢都 decentralize, 大家都唔會咁容易去 obey 權威或者法律, 變相就會容易有咗呢啲好踩界, 覺得係為咗伸張正義或者符合道德嘅行為。
>
> ("I feel that especially under the situation where the internet is so developed, a lot of things have become decentralized. Everyone is not so likely to obey authority or the law, and as a result, it becomes easier for these very borderline behaviors – seen as being for the sake of upholding justice or aligning with morality – to emerge.")

Respondent F's account employs normalization discourse that frames boundary-pushing doxxing behaviors as increasingly typical and socially acceptable. Lexical choices such as "好多嘢" ("a lot of things") and "大家" ("Everyone") invokes collectivization to present these practices as widespread and shared rather than exceptional. In addition, Respondent F attributes the rise of such behaviors to structural conditions like "decentralization" and the growth of the internet, which makes doxxing appear a natural consequence of social and technological advancement.

4.1.4 Disapproval: Ethical Concerns

Although the interview dataset shows a tendency to justify or normalize doxxing, one participant stands out in expressing clear ethical disapproval. Notably, the respondent does not primarily oppose doxxing on legal grounds, and in fact, none of the interviewees suggests doxxing was illegal, but instead, he emphasizes its moral implications. This creates a discursive space in which the boundaries of acceptable action are negotiated not through institutional discourse, but through personal ethical reflection.

> *Respondent D*: 我覺得係 immoral, 即係對我嚟講, 即係我會, 我覺得係同理心嘅問題, 即係一個人佢做呢一啲嘢之前, 佢有冇考慮過對於嗰個當事人會有啲咩傷害, 我覺得呢樣嘢唔單止係法律需要做嘅嘢 . . .
>
> ("I think it [doxxing] is immoral – that is, to me, I feel it's a matter of empathy. Like, before a person does this kind of thing, did they consider what kind of harm it might cause the person involved? I think this is not just something that the law should handle.")

Respondent D's disapproval is conveyed through a series of stance markers (Myers, 2012), notably the assertion "我覺得係 immoral" ("I think it's immoral"). The use of English for the keyword "immoral" amid the Cantonese sentence is noteworthy; code-switching here serves not only to emphasize the evaluative stance of the term doxxing, but also to mark it as socially or morally charged in a way that Cantonese alone may not sufficiently achieve. This declarative sentence without any hedging indicates the respondent's high degree of certainty. The repeated use of epistemic stance markers such as "我覺得" ("I think") and "對我嚟講" ("for me") further reinforces the speaker's personal positioning, asserting that individual moral awareness is more important than relying solely on legal regulation. This individual responsibility is further reinforced by the mentioning of "同理心" ("empathy"), framing doxxing in terms of ethics rather than the law. The rhetorical question "佢有冇考慮過對於嗰個當事人會有啲咩傷害?" ("did they consider what kind of harm it might cause the person involved?") functions as implicit critique of doxxers' behavior and an invitation to moral reflection. Respondent D continues:

> *Respondent D*: 即係我覺得需要立法嘅原因係因為 佢背後真係唔道德, 所以先需要立法, 但係我又覺得有好多時候 做咗立法呢一樣嘢嘅時候, 大家就會轉個法律嘅漏洞, instead of 去考慮返嗰件事背後道唔道德呢一樣嘢, 感覺大家嗰道德意識都會低咗。
>
> ("I think the reason legislation is necessary is because it's truly immoral at its core, that's why we need laws. But I also feel that once something becomes legislated, people would just shift their attention to legal loopholes instead of considering whether the act itself is moral or not. It feels like everyone's moral awareness becomes weaker.")

Respondent D explicitly establishes a causal relation between immorality and the need for legal intervention. However, this view is immediately problematized through contrastive framing, "但係 … 大家就會轉個法律嘅漏洞" ("people would just shift their attention to legal loopholes"), which reveals the limit of legal measures as insufficient in raising ethical awareness. While Respondent D's response is unique in its explicit opposition to doxxing, it exemplifies how alternative discourses, in this case, one that foregrounds morality over law, can potentially resist the dominant normalization of doxxing.

4.2 Ambivalence and Moral Tension

In the interviews, the participants were asked to reflect on the acceptability of notable doxxing cases in Hong Kong. A number of interviewees showed signs of *moral ambivalence* (Carr, 2009), in which they simultaneously endorsed doxxing practices and expressed their own ethical uncertainty. This moral ambivalence is not simply a sign of confusion or inconsistency, but, as Carr (2009) argues, reflects complex emotional and moral conflicts, and is an inevitable part of human experience. In the data, such moral ambivalence also allows participants to negotiate the moral conflicts between personal values and perceived social justice achieved by doxxing, as illustrated in Respondent K's words:

> *Respondent K*: 我理性上覺得所有人嘅私隱係要尊重, 但我覺得有啲人係值得畀人喺 law 以外去私人制裁佢。
>
> ("Rationally, I think everyone's privacy should be respected, but I think some people deserve to be privately sanctioned outside the law.")

The phrase 理性上 ("Rationally") illustrates what Reisigl and Wodak (2009) call perspectivization, that is, the expression of a speaker's involvement that positions their perspective. Here, the stance marker "rationally" signals

Respondent K's perspective and frames his viewpoint as being based on reason or logic. This logical perspective is contrasted with the more subjective judgment that follows, that some "deserve" private sanction outside the law. This contrastive framing allows Respondent K to acknowledge legal norms (protecting privacy) while simultaneously positioning certain individuals as morally exempt from them. Also using the term "rationally," Respondent S remarked:

> *Respondent S*: 可能滲透埋自己嘅一啲 ideology, 可能會話覺得起了一個開槍警嘅底係情有可原, 但理性上面就會覺得起底就係唔啱
>
> ("Maybe some of my ideology influences this. I might feel that doxxing a police officer who fired a shot is understandable, but rationally I know doxxing is wrong.")

The repetition of the modal of uncertainty "可能" ("maybe") and the self-reflection "滲透埋自己嘅一啲 ideology" ("some of my ideology influences this ... ") reveals the respondent's internal discursive struggle, where competing evaluations of doxxing coexist – one that sees doxxing as "understandable" in some situations, and another that is "wrong." By using hedging and self-reflection, Respondent S constructs a discourse that enables holding both positions to manage and negotiate ethical boundaries in digital contexts.

Ambivalence is often expressed through conflicted discourse. Respondent F noted:

> *Respondent F:* 其實我覺得我會好 resonate 到被起底嘅人, 但你話我支唔支持起底呢回事, 我係支持。
>
> ("I actually feel I can really resonate with people who are doxxed, but if you ask me whether I support doxxing – I do support it.")

This juxtaposition reveals the respondent's internal contradiction between empathy with victims and rational endorsement of doxxing. The emotional complexity is encapsulated in Respondent R's reflection:

> *Respondent R*: 即起底好似一個唔好嘅行為啦, 咁但係其實我都好開心喎, 即係佢係咪一件錯嘅事呢, 呢個係咪一個人性嘅黑面?
>
> ("So doxxing seems like a bad behavior, but actually I'm very happy. So 'Is it wrong? Is this humanity's dark side?'")

> *Respondent T*: 我都驚會造成傷害 ... 但同時我都會覺得 ... 咁咪好似警唔到世咁 ... 我都有唔同睇法, 兩面咁。
>
> ("I'm afraid it may cause harm ... but at the same time, if we don't doxx them, then it's like we can't warn society ... so I have different views, both sides.")

Both statements reveal the affective nature of ambivalence (Carr, 2009). Carr argues that expressions of moral ambivalence are often shaped by emotion, as divided feelings are crucial for how people experience and negotiate moral dilemmas. Respondent R's admission of happiness coexists with moral doubts, and Respondent T's fear of harm is coupled with the pragmatic function of doxxing. Respondent R's rhetorical questions ("Is it wrong? Is this humanity's dark side?") parallel Respondent T's explicit acknowledgment of ambivalence ("I have different views, both sides"). Structurally, the two statements follow a pattern of first presenting an ethical concern ("it may cause harm"), followed by an adversative conjunction ("but") [adversative], and ending with a competing justification ("warn society"). This discursive structure serves to balance ethics with subjective experience.

4.3 Morality and Legality in Doxxing

The analysis reveals a spectrum of attitudinal stances toward doxxing. These attitudes are often shaped by a competing discourse between morality and legality, where participants' shared notions of justice and accountability frequently override formal legal definitions of doxxing. In Section 3, the analysis of LIHKG posts reveals relatively homogenous legitimation discourse strategies to doxxing as a justified action to punish perceived wrongdoing. The interview data in this section demonstrate more diverse and ambivalent stances, where participants struggle with competing legal, moral, and affective discourses. On one hand, some participants legitimize doxxing through moral appeals to social justice ("伸張正義") and public interest ("公眾利益"); on the other hand, they openly acknowledge its potential to push moral boundaries. This ambivalence exemplifies dialogical tension (Bakhtin, 1981), where institutional legal discourse ("doxxing is illegal") clashes with grassroots discourse ("doxxing upholds justice"). This multiplicity and complexity of attitudes suggests that doxxing cannot be understood or interpreted through purely legal terms. As the next section demonstrates, institutional discourses often criminalize doxxing in terms of privacy violation and harm, overlooking the cultural pragmatics of shame and grassroots discourses of moral logics that sustain present-day digital vigilantism.

5 The Doxxing Law: Institutional Representations and Public Interpretations

This section examines the discursive mismatches between institutional representations of doxxing and how these are interpreted by the public. Institutional discourse in this study draws primarily from the official website of the Office of the Privacy Commissioner for Personal Data (PCPD), which includes a dedicated section on "Doxxing Offences," which outlines definitions of doxxing and the statutory provisions introduced through the 2021 amendment to the *Personal Data (Privacy) Ordinance* (PDPO). The PCPD is the statutory body responsible for enforcing data privacy laws in Hong Kong. It has the authority to investigate complaints, issue enforcement notices, and initiate prosecutions or refer cases to the police. Using survey data and follow-up interviews with university students in Hong Kong, this section explores how the law is interpreted in relation to official definitions. Through critical discourse analysis, the study identifies a number of conceptual and interpretive mismatches. This section briefly discusses the law's limited accessibility and the linguistic challenges of regulating digitally-mediated behaviors such as doxxing.

5.1 Awareness and Accessibility of the Doxxing Law

When it comes to the 2021 amendments to the PDPO that criminalized doxxing in Hong Kong, there is a significant gap between institutional efforts to define and legislate against doxxing and the public's understanding of what the law entails. Only 33 percent of the survey participants reported being aware of the doxxing law and the criminalization of doxxing. Participants were then shown the PCPD's definition of doxxing, and details of the scope of two-tier doxxing offences in the doxxing law, as quoted:

> Doxxing refers to the gathering of the personal data of target person(s) or related person(s) (such as family members, relatives or friends) through online search engines, social platforms and discussion forums, public registers, anonymous reports, and so on and disclosure of the personal data on the Internet, social media or other open platforms (such as public places). (PCPD, n.d.)

> (3A) A person commits an offence if the person discloses any personal data of a data subject without the relevant consent of the data subject—
>
>   (a) with an intent to cause any specified harm to the data subject or any family member of the data subject; or
>   (b) being reckless as to whether any specified harm would be, or would likely be, caused to the data subject or any family member of the data subject.
>
> (3B) A person who commits an offence under subsection (3A) is liable on conviction to a fine at level 6 and to imprisonment for two years.

(3C) A person commits an offence if—

    (a) the person discloses any personal data of a data subject without the relevant consent of the data subject—

        (i) with an intent to cause any specified harm to the data subject or any family member of the data subject; or

        (ii) being reckless as to whether any specified harm would be, or would likely be, caused to the data subject or any family member of the data subject; and

    (b) the disclosure causes any specified harm to the data subject or any family member of the data subject.

(3D) A person who commits an offence under subsection (3C) is liable on conviction on indictment to a fine of $1,000,000 and to imprisonment for five years.

(*Personal Data (Privacy) (Amendment) Ordinance*, 2021, s. 64)

Regarding the general definition of doxxing provided by the PCPD, 71 percent of the respondents find the definition to be clear or somewhat clear. Among the respondents who found the PCPD's definition of doxxing "unclear" or "somewhat unclear," some found certain key terms, such as "personal data" ambiguous. Others were unsure whether simply sharing publicly accessible information could still be considered illegal doxxing. Some expressed concerns regarding the lack of clarity about what constitutes intent. A number of participants suggested that the PCPD's definition is too broad or too subjective, leaving much room for misinterpretation.

When it comes to the two-tier offences, only 45 percent of the respondents found the two-tier law to be "clear" or "somewhat clear." However, this means over half of the respondents found the language of the law unclear and hard to understand. The respondents were asked to identify key reasons that might hinder their comprehension of the doxxing law (Table 3).

As indicated in Table 3, over 44 percent of the respondents considered the legal wording too technical, and 31.2 percent found some terms difficult, especially "*specified harm*" (指明傷害), "*intent*" (意圖), and "*personal data*" (個人資料), which seemed loaded and lacked clarity. Respondents who selected "Others" provided written explanations of why they found the law difficult to interpret. One respondent asked, 「指明傷害」指的是身體傷害還是精神傷害 ("Does 'specified harm' mean physical or mental harm?"); another stated, 傷害一詞過於含糊 ("Harm is too vague a term"); while another remarked, 意圖太廣泛，人人有不同理解 ("Intent is too broad – everyone understands it differently"). These

Table 3 Perceived barriers to understanding of the doxxing law

Reason	Number of respondents (*N* = 500)	Percentage (%)
Some of the words or phrases used are difficult to understand	156	31.2%
Some of the words or phrases are too technical	224	44.8%
The definition is too short	21	4.2%
The definition is too long	307	61.4%
The definition lacks concrete examples	170	34.0%
Other	16	3.2%

comments reveal semantic and lexical ambiguities of the law's language (see Section 5.2).

The perceived complex structure of the two-tier offence also hindered comprehension. 61 percent of the respondents said the law was "too long," and many struggled to differentiate first- and second-tier offences. One respondent wrote, "I don't know the difference between the first- and second-tier offences" (不知第一級和第二級的分別) ; another said, "It's hard to distinguish between tier one and tier two offences" (難以分別一級同二級罪行). Although a tiered structure is common in legislative drafting to enhance clarity and precision, in the case of the two-tier doxxing offences, the distinction between offences based on intent, recklessness, and actual harm caused was not obvious to readers. The language used in both tiers is highly similar and may fail to achieve its intended clarity. If these relatively educated university students struggle to understand the distinction, it is likely that less educated members of the public would find it even more challenging to determine what actions fall under which tier.

Some respondents also noted grey areas in the law, especially concerning re-sharing already publicly available personal data. In the open-ended comments in the survey, one respondent wrote:

> 如其個人資料本已被公開, 將其刊登在公共論壇又是否屬違法
>
> ("If personal data has already been made public, is posting it in a public forum still illegal?")

Similar uncertainties were also expressed by multiple interviewees. The law does not clearly and explicitly define what kind of personal data is protected once such information enters the public domain. Others mentioned the challenge of proving intent or recklessness. They also noted the lack of an objective standard for assessing intent and harm:

(1) 如何證實人是否有意圖進行一件事

("How do you prove someone intended to do something?")

(2) 受傷害的客觀標準

("What's the objective standard for harm?")

(3) 難以定義某些概念, 如實際指明傷害

("Some concepts like 'actual specified harm' are hard to define.")

Overall, these concerns emphasize the challenge in identifying and assessing subjective mental states and experiences like harm in the legal process. There is a broader disjunction between the technical and rather stringent requirements of the law and the public's understanding of these standards. With this background in mind, we turned to the interview data to probe more deeply into how participants made sense of legal definitions in practice. The discussion focuses on their interpretations of four key expressions found in official definitions and legal documents. The recurring keywords that were variably interpreted in the interviews are: "personal data," "intent," "harm," and "public interest."

5.2 Diverging Interpretations of Key Legal Terms in the Doxxing Law

5.2.1 Interpreting "Personal Data"

The concept of "personal data" is central to how doxxing is defined under the PDPO. The law criminalizes the unauthorized disclosure of such data under conditions likely to cause harm. Section 2.2.3 of the Ordinance provides the following definition of "personal data":

> In order to qualify as "personal data" under section 2(1) of the Ordinance, the data must relate directly or indirectly to a living individual and from which it is practicable to ascertain directly or indirectly the identity of the individual. Such data include, for instance, the name, identity card number, phone number, photo and residential address. The data should also be in a form in which access to or processing of the data is practicable. Otherwise, it falls outside the ambit of "personal data." (Personal Data (Privacy) (Amendment) Ordinance, 2021, s.2.2.3)

From an institutional perspective, the language used in this definition is intentionally broad and inclusive. Binomial expressions connected by conjunctions, as in "relate directly or indirectly," and "access to or processing ... is practicable," are adopted to broaden the scope of interpretation of various contexts where personal data may be shared. However, while this all-encompassing style of legal discourse allows for flexibility, it also introduces semantic vagueness that can confuse nonspecialist readers.

In the study, participants expressed uncertainty and confusion regarding what counts as "personal data." Many were skeptical that disclosing already-public information, such as social media profiles, would fall under the law. For these respondents, if someone has already shared their information publicly, it no longer counts as private and should not be protected by law (see also discussion in Sections 3 and 4).

> *Respondent K*: 已經講明係轉載一個屬於公開嘅資料嘅嘢，即係例如 forward 人哋嗰個 IG profile, 或者 Facebook 某條 link, 咁其實呢個已經係公開嘅, 咁即係個 post 係每個人都可以 access 嘅 information。咁你將呢一個 information 話畀人聽, 唔通咁樣都叫做起底咩?
>
> ("It's already clearly stated that it's just reposting something that's publicly available, like forwarding someone's IG profile or a Facebook link. That's already public, meaning it's information that anyone can access. So if you share this information with another person, how can that possibly be considered doxxing?")

This illustrates a discursive mismatch: the doxxing law's emphasis is on identifiability (whether direct or indirect), whereas the participant's focus is on privacy. In fact, many of the participants seemed to have equated "personal data" with *private* or *sensitive* information only, rather than data that could identify someone. As a result, they excluded widely accessible content from their understanding of what the law prohibits.

One controversial example of information frequently cited by the participants is car plate numbers. Though legally capable of identifying an individual, participants questioned whether such publicly visible identifiers should count as "personal data":

> *Respondent S*: 我覺得唔算係 expose 咗一個人嘅個人資料, 因為車牌就算我唔擺上網, 佢揸住架車週街行, 咁其實人人都見到㗎喇, 所以佢唔算係一個起底。
>
> ("I don't think it counts as exposing someone's personal data, because even if I don't post the license plate online, they're already driving the car around on the streets, so everyone can see it anyway. So I don't think that counts as doxxing.")

Some participants also raised questions about accuracy and truthfulness. They expressed uncertainty about whether sharing false or misleading information of an individual, such as a fabricated story about their past, still falls under legal protection:

> *Respondent S*: 但係會唔會有啲情況底下就係佢發布嘅資料佢以為係嗰個人嘅真實資料, 但其實唔係真嘅咁樣, 咁我就唔知。
>
> ("What if someone thinks the information they're posting is true, but it actually isn't? I really don't know what happens in that case.")

Taken together, these responses suggest a tension between institutional discourse and lay interpretation of "personal data." According to the law, "personal data" is narrowly or broadly defined in terms of the identifiability of data owners. If someone can be identified from the information, that information should be protected. However, the general public often interprets it in relation to context, whether the information is "private," and who owns the information. As the interviewees' statements suggest, nonspecialists tend to place more emphasis on the intention behind sharing the information and whether it was already publicly visible.

5.2.2 Interpreting "Intent"

According to the new amendments to the PDPO, doxxing becomes an offence when someone publishes others' personal data with "an intent to cause any specified harm." However, the PDPO does not define the legal meaning of intent or how it is measured. Some interviewees found the word "intent" problematic as it was unclear to them how intent was assessed. They also expressed concerns that intent could be easily misinterpreted by subjective judgments. Others critiqued the unclear boundary between acceptable and illegal intent, and how that would impact those who might unintentionally disclose others' data due to ignorance of the law.

> *Respondent R*: 點為之係有意圖咁樣起人底, 點樣有意圖地公開人哋資料, 佢冇講清楚。犯法嗰條線佢喺度定清楚
>
> ("What exactly counts as having the intent to doxx someone? What does it mean to deliberately publish someone's personal data? They haven't made that clear. The line for what's illegal isn't clearly drawn.")

Respondent F echoed the belief that without clear intent, liability should not be assumed:

> *Respondent F*: 不知者不罪
>
> ("Those who don't know [they are breaking the law] should not be guilty.")

Respondent F's belief "those who don't know should not be guilty" is noteworthy in that it directly challenges the long-standing legal maxim of "ignorance of the law is no excuse." This doctrine assumes that the general public should always understand the law, regardless of its complexity and accessibility. However, in reality, most people with no legal training would not reasonably comprehend legal discourse. Also, without a clear definition of intent in the PDPO, the interpretive burden falls upon both the lay public and prosecutors within the legal process. However, Kahan (1997) argues that the principle "ignorance of the law is no excuse" is less about punishing mere lack of knowledge and more about discouraging morally questionable behaviors such as malicious doxxing. Respondent F's belief reflects not only his lack of knowledge of the doxxing law but also a failure to align with shared moral values.

Some interviewees discussed scenarios in which content was originally posted for humorous or social purposes, but later evolved into something more serious, such as public shaming or vigilantism. These constant shifts of interpretive framework from one online discursive context to another, where meaning and intent are recontextualized by multiple layers of audience, were a recurring concern:

> *Respondent S*: 我諗到一個例子就係可能有啲人講笑佢 post 咗一個 video 上去，即係淨係想畀人笑下又好或者畀人欣賞都好，之後嗰個 post 下面就慢慢發展到係想起嗰個人嘅底同埋想識呢個人，無論係 positive comment 又好或者 negative comment 又好，咁係之後嗰啲人定係本身 post 嗰條片個人係起底呢？
>
> ("I can think of an example where someone might post a video just as a joke, either to make people laugh or for others to appreciate it. Then, in the comments section, things slowly develop into people wanting to dig up that person's background and find out who they are. Whether the comments are positive or negative, is it those later people who are doxxing, or was it already doxxing by the person who originally posted the video?")

Another participant raised similar concerns about seemingly light-hearted posts that nonetheless disclose identifiable information:

> *Respondent K*: 就算佢淨係想攞出嚟笑下。咁但係你真係攞咗人哋個 IG 出嚟，你真係畀咗人哋可能唔係好願意畀大家知嘅 information 出嚟，係囉，所以就算你變成乜嘢 form 都好，佢本身都係起咗人底。
>
> ("Even if it was just meant as a joke, if you really posted someone's IG and exposed information they probably didn't want shared, then no matter what form it takes, it's still doxxing.")

These quotes once again demonstrate the complexity of interpreting intent in digital contexts (see Yus, 2011), particularly on platforms like LIHKG, where communication is anonymous and subject to context collapse. In pragmatics, intention is neither always transparent nor directly accessible from the immediate linguistic context alone. According to speech act theory, there exist mismatches between a speaker's illocutionary act (intention) and the actual perlocutionary effect perceived by the hearer. This mismatch is further amplified in asynchronous communication channels like LIHKG, where interaction lacks nonverbal contextual cues. As Dynel (2021) observes, in one-to-many online interactions, the audience often projects meaning based on personal interpretation of utterances, not the speaker's intended state of mind. This dynamic is especially evident in the interpretation of what Dynel (2021) calls "jocular insults," that is, comments blending humor and hostility. Once recontextualized or reposted, the original intent of these jocular insults can be obscured entirely, making it difficult to distinguish serious insults from humor.

By contrast, legal frameworks often assume that intent is a straightforward, easily identifiable state of mind. However, in participatory digital spaces, intent is fluid, shaped by evolving contexts, audience, and reinterpretation. Durant and Leung (2017, p. 538) argue that legal interpretation must navigate between various forms of intention, including "the subjective, historical intention of an author," "the collective and cumulative intent of the legislature," and "intention modernized to fit contemporary norms." They further point out that "the scope of 'relevant context' within which any legal utterance or text is to be interpreted remains unclear" (p. 546), which reinforces the idea that meaning is not static. Applied to Hong Kong's doxxing law, relying strictly on "intent to cause harm" alone may lead to misjudgments of communication acts in a digital context. In digital spaces, the law cannot easily draw the line between what counts as friendly banter and malicious information disclosure. Using intent as a key criterion for distinguishing between legal and illegal doxxing is not easily operationalized in practice. For instance, an LIHKG user might post someone's personal information in a sarcastic comment together with a laughing emoji. Does this carry intent to harm? Is it a joke? Or is it merely information sharing? If a single emoji can be perceived as harmful, where should the line be drawn? (see also Danesi, 2021's discussion of "emoji forensics").

5.2.3 Interpreting "Specified Harm"

A third key term that generated confusion among participants was "*specified harm*," another core condition for criminal liability under the doxxing offences outlined in the amended PDPO. According to Section 64(6) of the PDPO:

"Specified harm" includes:

(i) harassment, molestation, pestering, threat, or intimidation to the data subject or their family;
(ii) bodily harm or psychological harm to that person;
(iii) harm causing that person reasonably to be concerned for their safety or well-being; or
(iv) damage to their property.

Despite this detailed breakdown of the various types of "harm," participants' open-ended comments in the survey reported that the meaning of "harm," and particularly how it would be assessed in legal terms, was unclear to them. As some survey respondents put it:

不清晰'指明傷害'的定義及意思

("The definition and meaning of 'specified harm' is unclear.")

"傷害"一詞過於含糊

("The word 'harm' is too vague.")

Beyond the lexical ambiguity of the word *harm*, participants were especially concerned with the practical application of the concept, particularly related to how the subjective feeling of harm could be measured, and what kind of evidence would be necessary to support a claim in court. A common concern among interviewees was that certain types of harm, especially emotional or psychological distress, are inherently subjective and difficult to assess:

Respondent K: 即係就算你搵一個例如 一個心理學方面嘅 professional 去 evaluate 當事人究竟有冇受到啲咩指明傷害, 呢啲都係一啲好主觀嘅嘢囉我覺得, 所以就會比較難去喺法庭上面大家講。

("Even if you brought in, say, a psychologist to professionally evaluate whether the person suffered any specified harm, I think that's still very subjective, so it would be hard to argue convincingly in court.")

Respondent R raised concerns about how intangible or nonphysical harm could be legally proven:

Respondent R: 我又會諗到呢啲係點樣證明, 尤其呢啲係 intangible 嘅嘢呢, 咁 prosecution 嘅時候究竟係點樣去證明的一件事, 呢個我都覺得有啲存疑有啲值得商榷嘅位。即係擔心呢啲係好 emotional, 好主觀嘅 perception, 咁我就覺得雖然係清楚咗, 但我覺得要證明傷害都係有一定難度。

("I wonder how you would prove this, especially when the harm is intangible. How would the prosecution go about proving it? I have doubts – it's very emotional and subjective. So even if the law is clearer, I think proving harm is still quite difficult.")

These responses reflect more than participants' confusion; they can also be interpreted as a form of resistance to legal definitions that appear overly rigid. These interviewees questioned not only how harm would be proved, but whether it should be constrained to one single meaning in the first place. Some expressed anxiety that the legal process might take people's words out of context, resulting in wrongful accusations. The phrase "reasonably to be concerned" is an additional point of ambiguity. It raises questions among participants about who determines what is *reasonable*, and by what measure.

Such concerns can be understood through the lens of *strategic lexicalization*, which Khafaga (2023) defines as "the selection of particular words through which specific intended meanings are represented in discourse" (p. 4). In the legal context, such lexical choices are purposeful, with the goal of limiting interpretive ambiguity. The term "specified harm," as well as the list of specified harms, serves to single out forms of harm that are seen as legally actionable. However, the very precision that benefits institutional actors may silence alternative scenarios. It sets boundaries around which harms "count." Participants' responses suggest that harm is not simply a matter of objective legal criteria but a deeply affective and subjective experience that cannot always be assessed through professional testimony or court procedures. This case illustrates the strength and limitations of strategic lexicalization in legislative drafting, in that while legal language can achieve precision and clarity, it can still marginalize alternative understandings of harm by prioritizing certain meanings while excluding others.

5.2.4 Interpreting "Public Interest"

In the legal discourse surrounding Hong Kong's anti-doxxing law, *public interest* (公眾利益) is a recurring yet ideologically contested term. What is interesting in the case of doxxing is that information disclosure is a double-edged sword – in that it can potentially cause harm and uphold justice at the same time. The term "public interest" therefore serves as a criterion for criminalizing doxxing and, paradoxically, as a condition under which doxxing may be lawfully defended, such as investigative journalism. In other words, "public interest" is inherently fluid and ambiguous, and its meaning shifts according to the ideological positions of those invoking it.

First, in government statements, especially those made during and after the 2019–2020 protests, public interest is used to support legal and institutional protection. In a blog post addressing the doxxing of police officers and their families, the then Secretary for Justice describes herself as the "guardian of public interest," stating that:

> Offenders are punished for the sake of public interest ... The immense public interest involved in protecting the due administration of justice as an integral component of the rule of law ordinarily calls for a deterrent sentence on the contemnor.

Here, public interest is aligned with the preservation of judicial integrity and institutional authority. This framing serves to legitimize the criminal prosecution of doxxing to maintain public order. By contrast, the same expression, *public interest*, specifically in section 64(4)(iv) of the PDPO, provides a legal defence for those charged with doxxing if they can prove that:

> the person disclosed the personal data solely for the purpose of a lawful "news activity" (or a directly related activity) ... and had reasonable grounds to believe that the publishing or broadcasting of the personal data was in the public interest.

At first glance, this reference to "public interest" may suggest a broader justification for personal data disclosure in some contexts. However, this scope is immediately limited through its alignment with legal and procedural domains, using words like "lawful," "authorized," "court order," and "legal proceedings."

In the interview data, *public interest* is understood and interpreted in very different ways by participants. Some respondents directly questioned the definability and authority of the term as constructed in law:

> *Respondent S*: 其實呢個口同鼻拗㗎喎, 即係我嘅認為所謂公眾利益當然係一啲, 如果好學術性咁講係會影響到公眾嘅一啲, 即係解完好似冇解過。
>
> ("This is all a matter of opinion. If you define 'public interest' academically, it's something that affects the public ... but once you try to explain it, it ends up meaning nothing.")

Respondent S continues:

> 即係我調返轉咁講, 有乜嘢唔係公眾利益啦
>
> ("Let me put it this way – what is not public interest?")

Other participants viewed the institutional use of public interest as rhetorically strategic, especially when weighed against citizens' attempts to justify doxxing with the same term:

Respondent K: 咁所以去到最後公眾利益本身呢一個字眼唔能夠好客觀地去界定清楚, 一定要配合返嗰件事, 再由個官就住個 context, 再 case-by-case 咁樣去 judge 返嚟。

("In the end, the term 'public interest' can't be clearly defined objectively. It has to be judged case by case, depending on the situation and context.")

Respondent R: 咩法例基礎都冇, 總之啲人佢哋一去公開啲資料就係話公眾利益... 咁我不如將計就計, 等政府你 charge 我... 解釋返點解我呢一個 case 彰顯緊嘅係一個公眾利益... 咁會唔會都係一個出路呢?

("There's no legal foundation—people disclose information and just say it's public interest... So maybe I'll just let the government charge me, and I'll defend myself in court by explaining why my case serves the public interest. Maybe that's the only way.")

Similar to the interpretation of "specified harm," these comments illustrate resistance to the strategic legal framing of "public interest" that, in public everyday use, remains quite subjective, open-ended, and context-sensitive. Respondents were also critical of the fact that its legal interpretation is placed solely in the hands of institutions.

Another participant suggested that failing to disclose harmful information could itself be a betrayal of public interest:

Respondent C: 如果我唔公開出嚟其實我係一個幫兇, 即係我係幫手去損害緊公眾利益, 公開出嚟先至係幫緊個社會

("If I don't make it public, then I'm complicit – I'm contributing to harming the public interest. Making it public is what helps society.")

Taken together, these accounts illustrate how *public interest* functions as an ideologically loaded discourse, often contested between institutional and public perspectives. While institutional actors deploy the term to justify criminalization and assert legal authority, participants mobilize it to challenge institutional power, recontextualize doxxing as a civic duty, and redefine the boundaries of justice from the bottom up (see also Section 4). The participants' resistance to the institutional framing reveals a fundamental tension of who gets to define the public and whose interests should be protected.

5.3 Discursive Tensions and the Limits of Legal Language

To sum up, this section has demonstrated the rather significant discursive mismatch between legal representations and public interpretations of doxxing. The findings suggest how legal discourse is shaped by and also shapes broader social norms and practices. While the law as communicated by the PCPD and the PDPO may appear precise through strategic lexicalization, such language use often leads to confusion, uncertainty, and resistance among the public. The analysis of four key legal expressions – *personal data, intent, specified harm*, and *public interest* – reveals the complex discursive space in which Hong Kong's doxxing law is interpreted, contested, and applied. Interview data suggest that these key terms are ambiguous and far from self-explanatory. It is clear from the data that the participants interpreted these expressions through every day, contextual, and pragmatic perspectives, rather than rigid legal definitions. This more fluid perspective results in varying and contested standards of what constitutes personal data, harm, and intent in real-life situations. The persistent discursive tension between legal and lay meanings is evident in the study. To address this, it requires not only better top-down communication and education of the law per se; policymakers should also be better informed of how legal discourse interacts with moral reasoning in everyday digitally-mediated communication.

6 Conclusions and Implications

6.1 Summary of Findings

This study has demonstrated that doxxing is not merely a technological or legal phenomenon, but also a discursive practice shaped by language, power, and ideologies. Through critical discourse analysis (CDA) of online forum posts, interviews, and legal texts, three key findings emerge:

– *Doxxing is discursively legitimized*: Doxxing is enacted and perpetuated by a moral economy (Thompson, 1971), a concept that is still guiding present-day global civil society and global social justice like digital vigilantism (Calabrese, 2005), where grassroots, communal notions of informal justice and morality may override formal legal frameworks. Both the forum discourse and interview participants consistently legitimize doxxing through discursive strategies like irony, (re)definition, blame attribution, and victimization. These strategies reflect a grassroots moral logic where privacy violations are seen as necessary resistance to perceived institutional insufficiency.
– *Ambivalence and ideological negotiation*: Attitudes toward doxxing reveal ambivalence, where participants simultaneously condemn doxxing as an

immoral act and justify vigilantism. This ambivalence is not mere uncertainty but a *dialogical tension* (Bakhtin, 1981) between institutional voices and informal justice seeking from the bottom up.
- *Everyday vs. legal meaning*: Keywords in the doxxing law, like "personal data," "intent," "harm," and "public interest," are reinterpreted through the lens of everyday, contextual, pragmatic meanings. When discussing doxxing motives, participants prioritize context over legal definitions, such as viewing car license plates as public data despite legal identifiability, or framing ironic praise as legitimate opinion. This mismatch suggests a fundamental tension between legal language that seeks static clarity and everyday discourse that is often more fluid and context-sensitive.

6.2 Doxxing and the Online-Offline Nexus

Doxxing illustrates what Blommaert (2019) describes as the "online-offline nexus," the idea that our social actions and identities are shaped across both digital and physical spaces (or what Lyons [2019] calls "phygital" spaces), which are now so closely intertwined that the online-offline dichotomy has become increasingly irrelevant. In this interconnected space, discursive actions online, such as doxxing and public shaming, can lead to consequences in the physical space, including harassment, threats, or even physical violence. As this study has shown, weaponized visibility (Trottier, 2017) in digital contexts can drive collective action and escalate harm beyond the screen. Context collapse (Wesch, 2009) allows content to be quickly reshared and reinterpreted by unintended audiences, who may recontextualize it from its original context and change its meaning and impact offline. For example, the doxxing of Hong Kong police officers' families, including the release of home addresses and details of children's schools, resulted in offline harassment, such as their children being bullied at schools.

The intertextual nature of doxxing, which repurposes personal data into oppositional narratives, creates what Androutsopoulos (2024) refers to as a "feedback loop." In this cycle, doxxing is often triggered by offline events, which then lead to physical world aggression, enacting and intensifying further verbal abuse and instances of doxxing online. For example, during the Hong Kong protests, the "DadFindBoy" Telegram channel, which gathered and exposed police officers' personal information, became a space for coordinating online doxxing, which allegedly led to offline confrontations (Lee, 2020). This case reveals that doxxing, as with many acts of online abuse, is rarely confined to one single online platform; instead, it spreads across multiple networked communities, gaining new meanings and reaching broader audiences as information gets circulated.

For forensic linguistics and discourse-based research of online abuses, the online-offline nexus presents some methodological challenges – *How can harmful intent be identified when discourse is scattered across digital and physical contexts?* and *How should harm be assessed when online discourse leads to offline consequences and vice versa?* The intertextual and recontextualized nature of doxxing (see Section 3.1), where the meaning of doxxing and its related practices can be easily reinterpreted to legitimize harmful actions, necessitates an analytical approach that takes into consideration the fluidity of context and meaning. In assessing harmful intent, researchers and investigators must focus not only on linguistic and discourse content within one single platform, but they should also trace the trajectories of meaning and intent as discourses are reinterpreted across media by different audiences.

6.3 Theoretical and Methodological Implications

This study brings to fore the crucial role of Critical Discourse Analysis (CDA) and pragmatics in understanding and responding to the complexities of doxxing in digital contexts. Legal drafting and communication often rely on static legal definitions and may overlook the fluid, context-dependent nature of digital communication. As this Element demonstrates, the anti-doxxing law in Hong Kong may be insufficient to uncover the covert discourse and pragmatic strategies used to legitimize doxxing, such as irony, euphemism, or "jocular insults" (Dynel, 2021), where intent is co-constructed by the writer and the intended audience rather than explicitly stated in the utterances.

By drawing on insights from CDA and pragmatics, the study reveals the limitations of legal *entextualization*, that is, extracting language from its original context and recontextualizing it within legal settings. This process may overlook the pragmatic complexity essential for interpreting discourse, and can distort or suppress the original meaning and voices of lay participants (Rock et al., 2013). For example, as shown in the data, discourses surrounding "public interest" are highly contested between institutions and lay members of the public, with the law using the expression to justify data protection, while lay actors reframe the same concept to defend doxxing and shaming. These discursive tensions reflect participants' ideological struggles over the legitimacy of doxxing, which is often shaped by culturally embedded norms such as "shame penalty" in Chinese societies, where public shaming functions as a mechanism of moral accountability (Chen, 2022).

Language is inherently ambiguous. Durant and Leung (2017) emphasize the importance of pragmatics in addressing semantic indeterminacy, implied and indirect meaning, and ambiguity of reference in legal interpretations. Pragmatic concepts like inference and co-text help resolve meaning uncertainty in linguistic evidence. For example, a case discussed in Durant and Leung involves the court inferring meaning in the defamation cases *Lord McAlpine v Sally Bercow*, where the interpretation of ironic utterances (e.g., "Why is Lord McAlpine trending? *Innocent face*") was central to determining whether a tweet was defamatory. The judge eventually ruled that the rhetorical question and the phrase "innocent face" conveyed a defamatory accusation. In the ruling, the court considered the contextual cues, audience's familiarity with the public figure concerned, and the news story on Twitter. Similarly, in the context of online doxxing discourse, the intended meaning of utterances can be easily manipulated or misinterpreted when taken out of their original context, especially with frequent use of covert discourse strategies. Coupled with CDA, pragmatic analysis becomes especially relevant in understanding digital communication, where context collapse can result in misinterpretation of speaker's intended meaning. In the actual investigation of online harmful discourse, audience reactions and interactive comments should also be analyzed alongside the questioned utterances. Such reactive comments often provide important contextual cues regarding how a message is perceived, amplified, or reinterpreted by readers. Pragmatic concepts such as speech acts, face, relevance, and (im)politeness can shed some light on investigating ambiguous cases, which could potentially be interpreted either as light-hearted remarks or covertly harmful comments, potentially triggering doxxing.

Finally, a key methodological finding that emerged unexpectedly from the research process itself was when multiple interview participants began to reflect ethically on their own stance and online actions. This reveals an unexpected and unintended dimension of participant engagement that warrants further theoretical consideration. As Respondents S and K reflect:

> *Respondent S*: 其實我對於起底真係零了解，其實都好坦白講，點解會參加呢一個 project 呢純粹都係因為見到有書卷，所以都冇特別去諗起底啱唔啱或者背後有啲咩嘢，去到 focus group 嘅時候先至知原來其他同學係咁諗㗎，我都冇諗過添，去到深少少就係 individual interview 㗎啦，去到啱啱..., 咦, 即係都會發現自己原來有啲地方係矛盾咗嘅咁樣。
>
> ("Actually, I really had zero understanding of doxxing. To be honest, the reason I joined this project was purely because I saw there was a book voucher, so I didn't really think much about whether doxxing was right or wrong, or what was behind it. It wasn't until the focus group that I realized other students had such thoughts – I hadn't thought about it at all. Then it went a bit deeper with the individual interview, and then just now ... eh, I realized that there are actually some parts where I myself am a bit contradictory.")

Respondent K: 我會出咗好多疑問囉做完嗰個 focus group interview 之後，例如頭先咁樣都問咗好多關於起底嘅嘢，我都會有疑問，都會有好多唔同嘅問號，因為如果你話係post片呀呢啲咁嘅行為，其實好多人都有做過，咁都有機會係起底。

("I came up with a lot of questions after the focus group interview. Like just now you asked me so many questions about doxxing. I had doubts and lots of question marks because if you talk about behaviors like posting videos, actually many people have done that, so there's a chance it could be considered doxxing.")

These reflexive comments reveal the values of focus-group interviews as both a research tool and a discursive site for self-examination. The multi-phased research design, from online survey, to focus group and one-on-one interviews – created unprecedented opportunities for the participants to examine their own assumptions and develop their critical awareness about their own and others' behavior as well as their language used online and offline. This also constitutes a form of research impact, where these young people, through engaging in the research project, enhance their awareness of the ethical and social consequences of doxxing, which fosters greater sensitivity to the harm it can cause.

6.4 Implications for Policy Communication

This study reveals significant gaps between official legal definitions and public understanding of doxxing in Hong Kong. Over half of the survey respondents found the PCPD's official definition unclear, with participants expressing confusion about key legal terms. Additionally, only 33 percent of the participants were aware that a specific doxxing law exists in Hong Kong and that doxxing could be criminalized. There is clearly a misalignment between policy intent and public understanding of the law. The findings also suggest that the participants hold ambivalent attitudes toward doxxing, seeing it as both a potential tool for justice-seeking and an immoral practice. This complexity suggests that existing policies need to enhance both legal language communication and public education on the issue.

(i) *Enhancing legal language clarity and education*: In promoting the implementation of anti-doxxing law in Hong Kong, the government should collaborate with the PCPD and adopt a more proactive approach to clarify potentially ambiguous legal expressions. This includes: (a) providing an annotated list of common types of personal data protected under the law; (b) explaining how "specified harm" is assessed; (c) clearly defining "intent" and explaining how it is interpreted in the legal process. Policy communication must move beyond the assumption that precision equals clarity. Future legislative drafting should incorporate plain language principles without compromising legal precision (Assy, 2011). This can include using concrete examples and accessible terminology to bridge the gap between institutional definitions and public understanding. Legal language education should also be integrated into the formal school curriculum, such as in Liberal Studies in Hong Kong. Beginning at the secondary or even primary level, common legal expressions and youth-friendly legal education should be introduced progressively. More broadly, comprehensive and regularly updated digital legal literacy programmes should be made compulsory from an early age. In Hong Kong, the Education Bureau should integrate legal literacy modules into existing curricula and establish partnerships between the PCPD and educators to co-develop age-appropriate legal education materials. A successful model in this regard is Singapore's National Digital Literacy Programme,[8] which includes "Digital Safety & Security" and "Digital Responsibility" competencies as key strands of digital literacy education. The Programme aims to address important areas such as understanding of online behavior, protection strategies, and ethical digital conduct. While education alone may not eliminate harmful discourse online, it plays a role in enhancing the public's critical thinking in both legal and media domains.

(ii) *Improving policy communication:* Currently, public education on doxxing and its legal implications in Hong Kong is primarily provided through the PCPD's website, press releases, radio APIs, and TV APIs. These relatively traditional channels, while informative, may not effectively reach the most relevant audiences, that is, active users of social media and local discussion forums where doxxing discourse is frequently produced. More direct engagement with digital media users is necessary for meaningful dialogues with those who are frequently exposed to or even engaged in doxxing discourses. The PCPD should also collaborate with schools and universities to develop educational programmes and awareness enhancement activities to encourage ethical reflections among young people, who are frequent users of these digital media and are particularly vulnerable to online harm.

The limited awareness of the doxxing law among participants indicates discursive gaps between policy communication and public perceptions. There is an urgent need to thoroughly examine public perceptions of the

---

[8] www.moe.gov.sg/education-in-sg/educational-technology-journey/edtech-masterplan/digital-literacy-and-technological-skills.

issue. Rather than relying solely on one-way, instructional communication channels such as websites, policymakers should create interactive platforms for public engagement with the ethical and legal dimensions surrounding doxxing and other harmful online practices. This could involve public forums and consultations, and collaborative definition-making processes that incorporate grassroots perspectives into legal discourse. The participants' ethical self-reflection in the present study suggests that dialogical policy processes could potentially be more effective than top-down communication campaigns.

(iii) *Integrating language-based research into policy development*: The value of language and discourse perspectives is clearly evident in this study, which has shown that doxxing is largely discursively constructed. The government should establish a task force with representatives from the PCPD and the Department of Justice, who would work closely with language and communication scholars. Further discourse-based research should be conducted within this task force to investigate multiple manifestations of online doxxing across digital platforms and the range of underlying motives and social conditions that shape doxxing practices. Drawing on tools and insights from CDA, this task force should systematically analyze known doxxing cases to identify recurring linguistic patterns and discourse strategies that legitimize or normalize unauthorized data disclosure.

(iv) *Support interdisciplinary research initiatives*: Research funding agencies should establish dedicated funding schemes to support interdisciplinary research on digital behavior. Bringing together legal scholars, linguists, psychologists, and media researchers, such interdisciplinary initiatives should explicitly recognize the role of language in constructing, sustaining, and justifying doxxing behavior. A good example in point is the EU-funded C.O.N.T.A.C.T. project (Assimakopoulos et al., 2017), which brings together scholars, NGOs, and stakeholders from various EU countries to collaboratively address discriminatory discourse and hate speech. The discourse analysts on the project team use CDA to systematically analyze harmful discourse in online news comments, with a particular focus on covert hate speech and implicit language such as irony. This kind of interdisciplinary work also contributes to the growing field of forensic linguistics, as it shows how systematic analysis of linguistic evidence in digitally mediated interactions can generate insights to inform legal interpretation and the investigation of online crime.

6.5 Final Thoughts and Future Research

This Element does not suggest that discourse or language analysis can offer a definitive method for identifying doxxing cases, nor does it claim to use language analysis to resolve the complexity of legal-ethical tensions surrounding doxxing. Rather, it contributes to conceptualizing doxxing practices as discursively constructed and sustained through strategic linguistic and discourse practices, a perspective that is often overlooked in the legal process. Insights from CDA reveal ongoing negotiation of ideologies surrounding doxxing, where the boundaries of public accountability and moral acceptability are constantly redefined. The critical analysis of discourse in this study also raises broader questions regarding power relations in digital governance, such as who has the right to define justice and whose interests should be protected in digital spaces.

This study, of course, has limitations, which in turn present opportunities for future research.

First, the study context is limited to Hong Kong only, and the data were collected from one platform (LIHKG). Target participants were exclusively university students in Hong Kong. The current study clearly serves as an exploratory case study to lay the groundwork for future research on doxxing discourses. A more comparative and comprehensive approach is recommended to examine doxxing discourse across cultural contexts with a more diverse range of participants. More broadly, the discourse of harmful research spreads across *polymedia* (Madianou, 2016). A polymedia environment is characterized as "the constant availability of a range of mediational tools for interpersonal communication" (Androutsopoulos & Stæhr, 2018, p. 119). For linguistics research, this concept is useful in tracing how people navigate and make meaning across multiple communication media. By documenting the discourse trajectories of doxxing within polymedia environments, researchers can better understand how platform affordances, user practices, and cultural norms interact to shape digital practices.

In terms of analytical approach, the study relies heavily on qualitative analyses of forum discourse and interview data. Future research can integrate computational methods to effectively complement qualitative discourse analysis. Researchers can employ corpus tools to examine much larger datasets of how discourses of doxxing circulate and evolve across multiple online platforms (e.g., in Hong Kong, from LIHKG to Telegram). Findings from corpus linguistic analysis could potentially inform AI model training that aims to detect patterns of covert harmful discourse.

Future research would also benefit from longitudinal research to trace how both public and legal discourses surrounding doxxing change over time. This could involve analyzing media reports, social media comments, or legal documents before and after major policy reforms to see how discursive strategies shift in response to new policy measures. Wodak's Discourse Historical Approach to CDA (Wodak, 2015) offers a valuable framework for such analyses, as it situates media texts within their broader historical contexts. Analyzing the discursive histories of doxxing would also shed light on its online-offline nexus (Androutsopoulos, 2024), as it situates online doxxing discourses within previous offline events, which in turn shape subsequent online doxxing practices.

Ultimately, the study of doxxing discourse is not just about identifying harmful language per se, but also about understanding how norms of ethics and justice are continuously negotiated in an increasingly mediated social world.

Appendix

1. **DISCOURSE STRATEGIES**

    1.1 **Affective Discourse:** Discursive actions aiming to provoke or express certain emotions.

        1.1.1 **Satisfaction**: Expressions conveying happiness or satisfaction with acts of doxxing.

        1.1.2 **Fear**: Expressions conveying fear toward doxxing targets.

        1.1.3 **Anger**: Expressions conveying frustration, resentment, or other emotional intensity in response to perceived wrongdoing or injustice.

            1.1.3.1 **Profanity**: Use of swear words or vulgar language to express anger.

            1.1.3.2 **Targeted anger**: Expressions showing anger directed at targets of doxxing beyond foul language.

            1.1.3.3 **Other**: Other expressions of anger that do not fall into the above categories.

        1.1.4 **Trust/Commitment:** Utterances showing commitment to doxxing, encouraging others to participate.

    1.2 **Legitimation**: Process of accrediting or licensing doxxing as acceptable social behavior (Reyes, 2011).

        1.2.1 **Rationalization**: Explaining doxxing by reference to goals or intended purposes (Van Leeuwen, 2007).

        1.2.2 **Authorization**: Using institutional voices (e.g., laws, official statements) to legitimize doxxing.

        1.2.3 **Doxxing as Self-Defense**: Framing doxxing as an act of protecting oneself or the community.

        1.2.4 **Re-definition (Doxxing as Not Illegal)**: Defining doxxing in moralized terms to claim it is not illegal (Van Leeuwen, 2007).

        1.2.5 **Intensification of Threats**: Exaggerating threats made by doxxed individuals, often via detailed or hyperbolic descriptions.

        1.2.6 **Self-Victimization**: Participants portray themselves as victims of alleged police misconduct (Lee, 2020).

        1.2.7 **Negative-Other Construction**: Attributing negative qualities to police officers (Lee, 2020).

- **1.2.8 Normalization**: Presenting doxxing as a normal, longstanding, or widely accepted practice.

1.3 Blame Attribution

- **1.3.1 Mitigation of Responsibility**: Replies reducing doxxers' blame by pointing out information was already public.
- **1.3.2 Denial of Responsibility**: Claims that doxxing was actually done by police against their own.
- **1.3.3 Manipulation of Institutional Voice**: Misuse or misunderstanding of laws to argue doxxing is legal.
  - **1.3.3.1 PDPO (Personal Data Privacy Ordinance)**: Incorrect beliefs, e.g., doxxing overseas is beyond government control.
  - **1.3.3.2 COIAO (Control of Obscene and Indecent Articles Ordinance)**: Referring to fellow members as friends to suggest COIAO doesn't apply to doxxing materials distribution.
  - **1.3.3.3 Others (Institutional)**: Other official sources, such as government press conferences.

1.4 Nomination (Referential): Labeling or categorizing social actors or groups (Wodak, 2015).

- **1.4.1 Dehumanization**: Representing people (mainly police) as animals or objects.
- **1.4.2 Pronouns**: Use of collective pronouns like "We" or depersonalizing terms.
- **1.4.3 Euphemism**: Using softer or indirect terms for doxxing.
- **1.4.4 Metaphor**: Using metaphors to represent groups, e.g., "dogs" for police.
- **1.4.5 Forum-Exclusive/Originated Slang**: LIHKG-specific slang terms (if unclear, coded under slang in lexical choices for further mapping).
- **1.4.6 On Actions/Events**: Nomination or referential acts applied to events rather than persons.
- **1.4.7 On Persons**: Nomination or referential acts applied to individuals.
- **1.4.8 Out-Group Membership Categorization**: Labeling groups as outsiders (e.g., police, government officials).
- **1.4.9 In-Group Membership Categorization**: Labeling groups as insiders (e.g., LIHKG users, Hongkongers).

2 LANGUAGE AND STYLISTIC CHOICES

- **2.1 Irony**: Remarks that literally sound like praise but are meant sarcastically.
- **2.2 Hyperbole**: Exaggerated descriptions, often of police violence.
- **2.3 Emoji:** Emojis used to signal sarcasm or to emphasize utterances.
  - **2.3.1 Sarcasm:** Emoji that indicates the whole reply as sarcastic.
  - **2.3.2 Emphasis:** Emoji to reinforce stance in utterance.
- **2.4 Forum-Exclusive Slang**: LIHKG-specific slang terms.
- **2.5 Pronouns**: Use of "We" or similar collective pronouns.
- **2.6 Other**: Additional stylistic devices.

3 INTERTEXTUALITY

- **3.1 Quotation:** Direct copying of earlier text.
- **3.2 Source (Parodying or Adapting):** Parodying or adapting known formats from other posts or texts.
- **3.3 Source Categories**
  - **3.3.1** General websites
  - **3.3.2** News sites
  - **3.3.3** Private messages on social media (Instagram, Facebook, WhatsApp, Telegram)
  - **3.3.4** LIHKG posts
  - **3.3.5** Government documents
- **3.4 Medium**
  - **3.4.1** Hyperlinks
  - **3.4.2** Images
  - **3.4.3** Direct text quotations

4 DEFINITION OF DOXXING

- **4.1 Types of Information Doxxed**
  - **4.1.1 Sensitive and Private Information**: Phone numbers, addresses of individuals or family members.
  - **4.1.2 Information in Public Domain**: Social media posts visible to all or leaked into the forum; publicly available info on officials.
  - **4.1.3 Hearsay**: Claims about knowing or hearing information about the person.
- **4.2 Distribution of Info on Entities**: Posts sharing info about non-person entities (not calling for further info search).

- **4.3 Built-in Forum Function**: Function archives previous posts/replies by a user to verify claims.
- **4.4 Comedic Effect**: Doxxing framed as sharing false info for humor within the community.
- **4.5 Disclosure of Personal Info**: Revealing info about individuals or groups.

5 SOCIAL ACTORS

- **5.1 General Public:** Ordinary citizens involved in doxxing.
  - **5.1.1 LIHKG users excluded**: Cases where only general public or netizens are involved, not forum users.
  - **5.1.2 LIHKG users included**: Cases where both forum users and general public are involved.
  - **5.1.3 LIHKG Users**: Forum members themselves.
  - **5.1.4 Members of Other Disciplined Services**: Police, fire services, medical personnel, and so on.
  - **5.1.5 Police Officers and Family Members**
  - **5.1.6 Government/Officials/Civil Servants**
  - **5.1.7 Privacy Commissioner:** Mention of privacy regulatory body.
  - **5.1.8 Mass Media**: Journalists and news outlets.
  - **5.1.9 Others**: Other actors like student leaders, politicians.

6 RECURRING THEMES

- **6.1 Policy Suggestions**: Proposals about doxxing laws from student interviews.
- **6.2 Validity of Info Doxxed**: Concerns about accuracy of exposed info.
- **6.3 Stigmatization of Doxxing**: Discussions about negative labeling of the term "doxxing."
- **6.4 LIHKG Culture**: Discussions about unique forum culture relating to doxxing.
- **6.5 Criminalization of Doxxing**: Talks about legal status, court injunctions.
- **6.6 Self-Reflection**: Interviewees' personal reflections on doxxing.
- **6.7 Shortcomings of Doxxing Law**: Opinions on improvements needed in public education or legal frameworks.
- **6.8 Reference to Other Malicious Acts**: Linking doxxing to harassment, intimidation, defamation, cyberbullying, and so on.
- **6.9 Uncertainties Toward Doxxing**: Expressions of doubt or confusion about doxxing.
- **6.10 Ambivalence Toward Doxxing**: Acknowledging both positive and negative aspects of doxxing.

Appendix

6.11 **Mismatch Between Illocution and Perlocution**: Differences between speaker's intended meaning and audience's interpretation.

6.12 **Intent**: Discussions about intention behind doxxing acts

6.13 **Illegal vs Immoral**: Debates on doxxing being legally wrong but morally acceptable, or vice versa.

6.14 **Legal Frameworks**

    6.14.1 **COIAO**: References to Control of Obscene and Indecent Articles Ordinance in relation to doxxing.

    6.14.2 **PDPO**: Discussions on Personal Data Privacy Ordinance.

6.15 **HARM (SPECIFIED)**

    6.15.1 **Harm in Institutional Voice**: Harassment, threats, bodily/psychological harm, damage to property.

    6.15.2 **Loss of Competitive Advantage**: Economic or tactical disadvantages suffered by doxxed individuals/groups (e.g., police losing tactical edge).

    6.15.3 **Loss of Credibility**: Exposure of dishonesty or immoral behavior reducing trustworthiness.

    6.15.4 **Loss of Legitimacy**: Loss of moral or legal authority through exposure.

    6.15.5 **Loss of Obscurity**: Removal of physical or social invisibility increasing vulnerability (Douglas, 2016).

    6.15.6 **Loss of Anonymity**: Revealing identity enabling further doxxing or harassment (Douglas, 2016).

6.16 **Gender**: Discussions linking gender and experiences of doxxing.

6.17 **Motives of Doxxing**

    6.17.1 **Disadvantaging**: Doxxing aimed at causing competitive or tactical loss.

    6.17.2 **Unintentional**: Doxxing due to carelessness without harmful intent.

    6.17.3 **Public Interest**: Releasing info believed to benefit public welfare or safety.

    6.17.4 **Retribution**: Doxxing to punish or seek informal justice against perceived wrongdoing (Anderson & Wood, 2021)

    6.17.5 **Other**: Other motives not categorized above.

6.18 **Public Interest (LIHKG)**: Forum posts justifying doxxing to expose misconduct or defend freedom of speech and right to know.

6.19 **Social Justice**: Discussions linking doxxing to concepts of justice and fairness.

References

Ademilokun, M., & Taiwo, R. (2013). Discursive strategies in newspaper campaign advertisements for Nigeria's 2011 elections. *Discourse & Communication*, *7*(4), 435–455. https://doi.org/10.1177/1750481313494501.

Amnesty International. (2019). How not to police a protest: Unlawful use of force by Hong Kong police. www.amnesty.org/download/Documents/ASA1705762019ENGLISH.pdf.

Anderson, J., & Wood, J. (2021). Doxxing: A conceptual framework. *New Media & Society*, *23*(1), 203–220.

Androutsopoulos, J. (2008). Potentials and limitations of discourse-centred online ethnography. *Language@ internet*, 5.

Androutsopoulos, J. (2010). Localizing the global on the participatory web. In N. Coupland (ed.), *The handbook of language and globalization* (pp. 201–231). Blackwell.

Androutsopoulos, J. (2014). Moments of sharing: Entextualization and linguistic repertoires in social networking. *Journal of Pragmatics*, *73*, 4–18.

Androutsopoulos, J. (2024). The Offline–Online Nexus. *The Bloomsbury Handbook of Linguistic Landscapes*, 441–455.

Androutsopoulos, J., & Stæhr, A. (2018). Moving methods online: Researching digital language practices. In A. Creese & A. Blackledge (eds.), *The Routledge handbook of language and superdiversity* (pp. 118–132). Routledge.

Assimakopoulos, S., Baider, F. H., & Millar, S. (2017). *Online hate speech in the European Union: A discourse-analytic perspective.* Springer Nature.

Assy, R. (2011). Can the law speak directly to its subjects? The limitation of plain language. *Journal of Law and Society*, *38*(3), 376–404.

Badarneh, M. A. (2020). "Like a donkey carrying books" Intertextuality and impoliteness in Arabic online reader responses. *Journal of Language Aggression and Conflict*, *8*(1), 1–28.

Baider, F., & Constantinou, M. (2020). Covert hate speech: A contrastive study of Greek and Greek Cypriot online discussions with an emphasis on irony. *Journal of Language Aggression and Conflict*, *8*(2), 262–287.

Bakhtin, M. M. (1981). *The dialogic imagination: Four essays.* University of Texas Press.

Blommaert, J. (2019). From groups to actions and back in online-offline sociolinguistics. *Multilingua*, *38*(4), 485–493.

Bandura, A., Barbaranelli, C., Caprara, G. V., & Pastorelli, C. (1996). Mechanisms of moral disengagement in the exercise of moral agency. *Journal of Personality and Social Psychology, 71*(2), 364–374.

Barton, D., & Lee, C. (2013/2025). *Language online: Investigating digital texts and practices*. Routledge.

Bergmann, J. R. (1998). Introduction: Morality in discourse. *Research on Language & Social Interaction, 31*(3–4), 279–294. https://doi.org/10.1080/08351813.1998.9683594.

Bhatia, V. K. (2010). Legal writing: Specificity Specification in legislative writing: Accessibility, transparency, power and control. In M. Coulthard & A. Johnson (eds.), *The Routledge handbook of forensic linguistics* (pp. 65–78). Routledge.

Binckes, J. (2022, December 15). What is doxxing? Elon Musk claims he was doxxed by the journalists suspended Thursday by Twitter. *MarketWatch*. www.marketwatch.com/story/what-is-doxxing-elon-musk-claims-he-was-doxxed-by-the-journalists-suspended-thursday-by-twitter-11671222702.

Bouvier, G., & Machin, D. (2020). Critical discourse analysis and the challenges and opportunities of social media. In S. M. Guillem & C. Toula (eds.), *Critical discourse studies and/in communication* (pp. 39–53). Routledge.

boyd, d. (2010). "Social network sites as networked publics: Affordances, dynamics, and implications." In Z. Papacharissi (ed.), *Networked self: Identity, community, and culture on social network sites* (pp. 47–66). Routledge.

Calabrese, A. (2005). Communication, global justice and the moral economy. *Global Media and Communication, 1*(3), 301–315.

Carr, D. (2009). Virtue, mixed emotions and moral ambivalence. *Philosophy, 84*(1), 31–46.

Chen, Q., Chan, K., & Cheung, A. (2018). Doxing victimization and emotional problems among secondary school students in Hong Kong. *International Journal of Environmental Research and Public Health, 15*(12), 1–8. https://doi.org/10.3390/ijerph15122665.

Chen, Q., Chan, K. L., & Cheung, A. S. Y. (2019). Doxing: What adolescents look for and their intentions. *International Journal of Environmental Research and Public Health, 16*(2), 1–14. https://doi.org/10.3390/ijerph16020218.

Chen, X. (2002). Social control in China: Applications of the labeling theory and the reintegrative shaming theory. *International Journal of Offender Therapy and Comparative Criminology, 46*(1), 45–63.

References

Cheong, P. H., & Gong, J. (2010). Cyber vigilantism, transmedia collective intelligence, and civic participation. *Chinese Journal of Communication*, *3*(4), 471–487.

Cheung, A. (2021). Doxing and the challenge to legal regulation: When personal data become a weapon. In J. Bailey, A. Flynn, & N. Henry (eds.), *The Emerald international handbook of technology-facilitated violence and abuse* (pp. 577–594). Emerald.

Chouliaraki, L. (2016). Victimhood, voice, and power in digital media. In K.-M. Simonsen & J. R. Kjaergard (eds.), *Discursive framings of human rights* (pp. 267–284). Birkbeck Law Press.

Choy, J. (2020). *Umbrella uprising: A visual documentation of the 2019 Hong Kong protests*. Jeffrey Choy.

Clark, M. D. (2020). DRAG THEM: A brief etymology of so-called "cancel culture". *Communication and the Public*, *5*(3–4), 88–92.

Cremins, D. (2024). Defending the public quad: Doxxing, campus speech policies, and the First Amendment. *Stanford Law Review*, *76*, 1813–1835. https://review.law.stanford.edu/wp-content/uploads/sites/3/2024/10/Cremins-76-Stan.-L.-Rev.-1813.pdf.

Crespo-Fernández, E. (2018). Euphemism as a discursive strategy in US local and state politics. *Journal of Language and Politics*, *17*(6), 789–811.

Cross, C. (2015). No laughing matter: Blaming the victim of online fraud. *International Review of Victimology*, *21*(2), 187–204.

Crown Prosecution Service. (2024, July 15). *Cybercrime – prosecution guidance*. www.cps.gov.uk/legal-guidance/cybercrime-prosecution-guidance.

Danesi, M. (2021). The law and emojis: Emoji forensics. *International Journal for the Semiotics of Law-Revue internationale de Sémiotique juridique*, *34*, 1117–1139.

Douglas, D. M. (2016). Doxing: A conceptual analysis. *Ethics and Information Technology*, *18*(3), 199–210.

Durant, A., & Leung, J. H. (2017). Pragmatics in legal interpretation. In A. Barron, Y. Gu, & G. Steen (eds.), *The Routledge Handbook of Pragmatics* (pp. 535–549). Routledge.

Dynel, M. (2021). Desperately seeking intentions: Genuine and jocular insults on social media. *Journal of Pragmatics*, *179*, 26–36.

Fairclough, N. (1992). *Discourse and social change*. Polity Press.

Fairclough, N. (2001). Critical discourse analysis as a method in social scientific research. *Methods of Critical Discourse Analysis*, *5*(11), 121–138.

Fairclough, N. (2003). *Analysing discourse*. Routledge.

Feltwell, T., Vines, J., Salt, K., et al. (2017). Counter-discourse activism on social media: The case of challenging "poverty porn" television. *Computer*

Supported Cooperative Work (CSCW), *26*(3), 345–385. https://doi.org/10.1007/s10606-017-9275-z.

Forsyth, A. (2020). The protestors and the Hong Kong police force – Doxxing of personal data. GALA. http://blog.galalaw.com/post/102g3n5/the-protestors-and-the-hong-kong-police-force-doxxing-of-personal-data.

Foucault, M. (1971). Orders of discourse. *Social Science Information*, *10*(2), 7–30.

Foucault, M. (1972). *Archaeology of knowledge*. Tavistock.

Galleguillos, S. (2022). Digilantism, discrimination, and punitive attitudes: A digital vigilantism model. *Crime, Media, Culture*, *18*(3), 353–374.

Gao, L. (2016). The emergence of the human flesh search engine and political protest in China: Exploring the Internet and online collective action. *Media, Culture & Society*, *38*(3), 349–364.

Garcés-Conejos Blitvich, P. (2021). Getting into the mob: A netnographic, case study approach to online public shaming. In M. Johansson, S. K. Tanskanen, & J. Chovanec (eds.), *Analyzing digital discourses* (pp. 247–276). Springer. https://doi.org/10.1007/978-3-030-84602-2_10.

Garcés-Conejos Blitvich, P. (2022). Moral emotions, good moral panics, social regulation, and online public shaming. *Language & Communication*, *84*, 61–75.

Götz, N. (2015). "Moral economy": Its conceptual history and analytical prospects. *Journal of Global Ethics*, *11*(2), 147–162.

Hansson, S., & Page, R. (2024). Discourses of political blame games: Introduction. *Discourse, Context & Media*, *60*, 1–4.

Hardaker, C. (2013). "Uh . . . . not to be nitpicky, but . . . the past tense of drag is dragged, not drug.": An overview of trolling strategies. *Journal of Language Aggression and Conflict*, *1*(1), 58–86.

Hart, C. (2021). Animals vs. armies: Resistance to extreme metaphors in anti-immigration discourse. *Journal of Language and Politics*, *20*(2), 226–253.

Herring, S. (1999). The rhetorical dynamics of gender harassment on-line. *The Information Society*, *15*(3), 151–167.

Hodsdon-Champeon, C. (2010). Conversations within conversations: Intertextuality in racially antagonistic online discourse. *Language@ internet*, *7*, 1–22.

Hong Kong Free Press (HKFP). (2023). Hong Kong woman handed 2-month suspended sentence over doxxing alleged scammer. https://hongkongfp.com/2023/03/08/hong-kong-woman-handed-2-month-suspended-sentence-over-doxxing-alleged-scammer/.

Huey, L., Ferguson, L., & Towns, Z. (2025). "Cops need doxxed": Releasing personal information of police officers as a tool of political harassment. *Crime & Delinquency, 71*(3), 714–739.

John, A., Glendenning, A. C., Marchant, A., et al. (2018). Self-harm, suicidal behaviours, and cyberbullying in children and young people: Systematic review. *Journal of Medical Internet Research, 20*(4), e9044.

Kagan, M., Kagan, M., Pinson, H., & Schler, L. (2019). No policies and no politics: Israeli teachers, asylum seeker pupils, and remobilized strategies of avoidance and depoliticization. *Race Ethnicity and Education, 25*(1), 1–19.

Kahan, D. M. (1997). Ignorance of law in an excuse–but only for the virtuous. *Michigan Law Review, 96*, 127–154.

Khafaga, A. (2023). Strategic lexicalization in courtroom discourse: A corpus-assisted critical discourse analysis. *Cogent Arts & Humanities, 10*(1), 1–27.

Khan, S. (2024, December 16). Australia: New privacy legislation criminalizes doxxing. *Global Legal Monitor.* www.loc.gov/item/global-legal-monitor/2024-12-16/australia-new-privacy-legislation-criminalizes-doxxing/.

KhosraviNik, M. (ed.). (2023). *Social Media and Society: Integrating the digital with the social in digital discourse* (Vol. 100). John Benjamins.

KhosraviNik, M., & Unger, J. W. (2016). Critical discourse studies and social media: Power, resistance and critique in changing media ecologies. *Methods of Critical Discourse Studies, 3*, 205–233.

Koller, V. (2020). Analysing metaphor in discourse. In C. Hart (ed.), *Researching discourse* (pp. 77–96). Routledge.

Krzyżanowski, M. (2020). Normalization and the discursive construction of "new" norms and "new" normality: Discourse in the paradoxes of populism and neoliberalism. *Social Semiotics, 30*(4), 431–448.

Lambert, S. D., & Loiselle, C. G. (2008). Combining individual interviews and focus groups to enhance data richness. *Journal of Advanced Nursing, 62*(2), 228–237.

Lee, C. (2020). Doxxing as discursive action in a social movement. *Critical Discourse Studies, 19*(3), 326–344.

Leung, H. (2019, September 6). A glossary of Hong Kong protest slang. *Time.* April 9, 2025. https://time.com/5668286/hong-kong-protests-slang-language-cantonese-glossary/.

Lyons, K. (2019). Let's get phygital: Seeing through the 'filtered' landscapes of Instagram. *Linguistic Landscape, 5*(2), 179–197.

Madianou, M. (2016). Ambient co-presence: Transnational family practices in polymedia environments. *Global Networks, 16*(2), 183–201.

Maragkou, E. (2019). "Dadfindboy": How activists in Hong Kong are hijacking state tools of surveillance. *University of Amsterdam.*

Matza, D., & Sykes, G. (1957). Techniques of neutralization: A theory of delinquency. *American Sociological Review, 22*(6), 664–670.

Mauran, C. (2022, December 16). EU says sanctions are coming after Elon Musk suspends journalists from Twitter. *Mashable.* https://mashable.com/article/elon-musk-european-union-sanction-twitter-suspending-journalists.

Murumaa-Mengel, M., & Muuli, L. M. (2021). Misogynist content exposé pages on Instagram: Five types of shamings, moderators and audience members. *Participations: Journal of Audience and Reception Studies, 18*(2), 100–123.

Myers, G. (2012Stance-taking and public discussion in blogs. In L. Chouliaraki (ed.), *Self-mediation* (pp. 55–67). Routledge.

Nott, L. (2025, May 12). What is doxing and is doxing illegal? Everything you should know. *Freedom Forum.* www.freedomforum.org/is-doxing-illegal/.

Oddo, J. (2011). War legitimation discourse: Representing 'us' and 'them' in four US presidential addresses. *Discourse & Society, 22*(3), 287–314. https://doi.org/10.1177/0957926510395442.

PCPD. (2020). "Weaponization of personal data and duty of social media" – Privacy Commissioner's article contribution at Hong Kong Lawyer, PCPD. https://www.pcpd.org.hk/english/news_events/newspaper/newspaper_202001.html.

Privacy Commissioner for Personal Data (PCPD) (n.d.). Doxxing. www.pcpd.org.hk/english/doxxing/index.html.

Parliament of Australia. (2024). *Privacy and Other Legislation Amendment Act 2024.* https://parlinfo.aph.gov.au/parlInfo/search/display/display.w3p;db=LEGISLATION;id=legislation%2Fbills%2Fr7249_aspassed%2F0003;query=Id%3A%22legislation%2Fbills%2Fr7249_aspassed%2F0000%22.

Phillips, W. (2015). *This is why we can't have nice things: Mapping the relationship between online trolling and mainstream culture.* MIT Press.

Reisigl, M., & Wodak, R. (2009). The discourse-historical approach (DHA). In R. Wodak & M. Meyer (eds.), *Methods for critical discourse analysis* (2nd ed., pp. 87–121). Sage.

Reyes, A. (2011). Strategies of legitimation in political discourse: From words to actions. *Discourse & Society, 22*(6), 781–807. https://doi.org/10.1177/0957926511419927.

Rheindorf, M. (2019). *Revisiting the toolbox of discourse studies: New trajectories in methodology, open data, and visualization.* Springer International Publishing.

Rock, F., Heffer, C., & Conley, J. M. (2013). Textual travel in legal–lay communication. In F. Rock, C. Heffer, & J. M. Conley (eds.), *Legal-lay communication: Textual travels in the law* (pp. 3–32). Oxford University Press.

SCMP. (2019). Hong Kong privacy watchdog wants more power battle doxxing. https://www.scmp.com/news/hong-kong/politics/article/3036046/hong-kong-privacy-watchdog-wants-more-powerbattle-doxxing.

Skoric, M. M., Wong, K. H., Chua, J. P. E., Yeo, P. J., & Liew, M. A. (2010). Online shaming in the Asian context: Community empowerment or civic vigilantism? *Surveillance & Society, 8*(2), 181–199. https://doi.org/10.24908/ss.v8i2.3485.

South China Morning Post (SCMP) (2023). Hong Kong's privacy watchdog arrests woman, 27, for suspected doxxing after she allegedly posted personal details of friend's ex-boyfriend online, www.scmp.com/news/hong-kong/law-and-crime/article/3217625/hong-kongs-privacy-watchdog-arrests-woman-27-suspected-doxxing-after-she-allegedly-posted-personal.

Sykes, G. M., & Matza, D. (2017). Techniques of neutralization: A theory of delinquency. In T. G. Blomberg, F. T. Cullen, C. Carlsson, & C. L. Jonson (eds.), *American sociological review*, Volume 21 (pp. 33–41). Routledge.

Teo, P. (2000). Racism in the news: A critical discourse analysis of news reporting in two Australian newspapers. *Discourse & Society, 11*(1), 7–49.

Thompson, E. P. (1971). The moral economy of the English crowd in the eighteenth century. *Past & Present, 50*(1), 76–136.

Trottier, D. (2017). Digital vigilantism as weaponisation of visibility. *Philosophy & Technology, 30*, 55–72.

van Dijk, T. (2009). Critical discourse studies: A sociocognitive approach. *Methods of Critical Discourse Analysis, 2*(1), 62–86.

Van Dijk, T. A. (1998). Opinions and ideologies in the press. In A. Bell & P. Garrett (eds.), *Approaches to media discourse* (pp. 21–63). Blackwell.

Van Leeuwen, T. (2007). Legitimation in discourse and communication. *Discourse & Communication, 1*(1), 91–112.

Van Leeuwen, T. (2009). Discourse as the recontextualization of social practice: A guide. In R. Wodak & M. Meyer (eds.), *Methods of critical discourse analysis* (2nd ed., pp. 144–161). Sage.

Van Leeuwen, T., & Wodak, R. (1999). Legitimizing immigration control: A discourse-historical analysis. *Discourse Studies, 1*(1), 83–118.

Wauters, K., Lievens, B., & Valcke, P. (2014). Privacy awareness and online behavior: A study of European teenagers. *Information & Computer Security, 22*(1), 47–64.

Wesch, M. (2009). An anthropological introduction to YouTube. *Visual Anthropology Review*, *25*(2), 169–185.

Wodak, R. (1990). Discourse analysis: Problems, findings, perspectives. *Text-Interdisciplinary Journal for the Study of Discourse*, *10*(1–2), 125–132. https://doi.org/10.1515/text.1.1990.10.1-2.125.

Wodak, R. (1995). The development and forms of racist discourse in Austria since 1989. In D. Graddol & S. Thomas (eds.), *Language in a changing Europe* (pp. 1–15). British Association for Applied Linguistics and Multilingual Matters.

Wodak, R. (2001). The discourse-historical approach. In R. Wodak & M. Meyer (eds.), *Methods of critical discourse analysis* (pp. 63–94). Sage.

Wodak, R. (2007). Pragmatics and critical discourse analysis: A cross-disciplinary inquiry. *Pragmatics & Cognition*, *15*(1), 203–225.

Wodak, R. (2014). Critical discourse analysis. In C. Leung & B. V. Street (eds.), *The Routledge companion to English studies* (pp. 302–316). Routledge.

Wodak, R. (2015). Critical discourse analysis, discourse-historical approach. *The international encyclopedia of language and social interaction*, *3*.

Wodak, R., & Meyer, M. (2009). Critical discourse analysis: History, agenda, theory and methodology. In R. Wodak & M. Meyer (eds.), *Methods of critical discourse analysis* (2nd ed., pp. 1–33). Sage.

Wodak, R., & Meyer, M. (eds.). (2015). *Methods of critical discourse studies*. Sage.

Wong, C. K. (2024). Navigating gender hate in manospheres: Women's affective dissonance and refusal on LIHKG in the 2019 Hong Kong anti-extradition bill movement. *Communication, Culture & Critique*, *17*(2), 112–119.

Yus, F. (2011). *Cyberpragmatics: Internet-mediated communication in context*. John Benjamins.

Acknowledgments

I would like to thank the series editors, Tim Grant and Tammy Gales, for their support and patience throughout the development of this Element. I am also grateful to the two anonymous reviewers for their constructive feedback on an earlier draft of the manuscript. This project was made possible through funding from the Public Policy Research Funding Scheme (Ref. 2021.A4.075.21A) and the Hong Kong Research Grants Council General Research Fund (Ref. 14604323), which supported parts of the research on which this manuscript is based. I am indebted to my research assistants Wayne Kwong and Szeto Hiu-Yuet for their dedicated support in data collection and analysis. I would also like to acknowledge Christoph Hafner and Dennis Chau for their involvement in developing early ideas of the project. Most importantly, I thank the research participants of the two projects for generously sharing their time and data.

Cambridge Elements

Forensic Linguistics

Tim Grant
Aston University

Tim Grant is Professor of Forensic Linguistics, Director of the Aston Institute for Forensic Linguistics, and past president of the International Association of Forensic Linguists. His recent publications have focussed on online sexual abuse conversations including *Language and Online Identities: The Undercover Policing of Internet Sexual Crime* (with Nicci MacLeod, Cambridge, 2020).

Tim is one of the world's most experienced forensic linguistic practitioners and his case work has involved the analysis of abusive and threatening communications in many different contexts including investigations into sexual assault, stalking, murder, and terrorism. He also makes regular media contributions including presenting police appeals such as for the BBC Crimewatch programme.

Tammy Gales
Hofstra University

Tammy Gales is Professor of Linguistics and the Director of Research at the Institute for Forensic Linguistics, Threat Assessment, and Strategic Analysis at Hofstra University, New York. She has served on the Executive Committee for the International Association of Forensic Linguists (IAFL), is on the editorial board for the peer-reviewed journals Applied Corpus Linguistics and Language and Law / Linguagem e Direito, and is a member of the advisory board for the BYU Law and Corpus Linguistics group. Her research interests cross the boundaries of forensic linguistics and language and the law, with a primary focus on threatening communications. She has trained law enforcement agents from agencies across Canada and the U.S. and has applied her work to both criminal and civil cases.

About the Series

Elements in Forensic Linguistics provides high-quality accessible writing, bringing cutting-edge forensic linguistics to students and researchers as well as to practitioners in law enforcement and law. Elements in the series range from descriptive linguistics work, documenting a full range of legal and forensic texts and contexts; empirical findings and methodological developments to enhance research, investigative advice, and evidence for courts; and explorations into the theoretical and ethical foundations of research and practice in forensic linguistics

Cambridge Elements

Forensic Linguistics

Elements in the Series

A Theory of Linguistic Individuality for Authorship Analysis
Andrea Nini

Forensic Linguistics in Australia: Origins, Progress and Prospects
Diana Eades, Helen Fraser and Georgina Heydon

Online Child Sexual Grooming Discourse
Nuria Lorenzo-Dus, Craig Evans and Ruth Mullineux-Morgan

Spoken Threats from Production to Perception
James Tompkinson

Authorship Analysis in Chinese Social Media Texts
Shaomin Zhang

The Language of Romance Crimes: Interactions of Love, Money, and Threat
Elisabeth Carter

Legal-Lay Discourse and Procedural Justice in Family and County Courts
Tatiana Grieshofer

Forensic Linguistics in China: Origins, Progress, and Prospects
Yuan Chuanyou, Xu Youping and Lu Nan

Decoding Terrorism: An Interdisciplinary Approach to a Lone-Actor Case
Julia Kupper, Marie Bojsen-Møller, Tanya Karoli Christensen, Dakota Wing, Marcus Papadopulos and Sharon Smith

Forensic Linguistics in Southern Africa: Origins, Progress, and Prospects
Russell H. Kaschula, Monwabisi K. Ralarala, Eliseu Mabasso, Zakeera Docrat, Wellman Kondowe and Paul Svongoro

Trust, Discourse, and Corporate Corruption: The Case of Enron
Matteo Fuoli, Adam Nix, Alicia Wickert and Annina Van Riper

Doxxing Discourse
Carmen Lee

A full series listing is available at: www.cambridge.org/EIFL

For EU product safety concerns, contact us at Calle de José Abascal, 56–1°,
28003 Madrid, Spain or eugpsr@cambridge.org.

www.ingramcontent.com/pod-product-compliance
Lightning Source LLC
LaVergne TN
LVHW011853060526
838200LV00054B/4303